Table of Co

Table of Contents 1

Warning 5

Disclaimer 6

Copyright 7

Dedications 8

1 BUCKLED LEGS 9

2 THEY'RE NOT STEALING 11

3 MICHAEL'S MUSIC LESSONS 18

4 WHY I'M STOOD BY THE DOOR 21

5 MARK WILLIS FLASHBACK 25

6 MORNING SUNSHINE 28

7 BRAVE AND FEARLESS 31

8 THE ONLY HELP 33

9 ACT NOW 34

10 THE BULLY REVEALED 35

11 FIGHTING INSTRUCTIONS 38

12 IT'S TIME TO FIGHT 40

13 THE SHIRT 43

14 UNSTOPPABLE 46

15 JABS AND THE AFTERMATH 50

16 TRUMPET SOLO 53

17 MUM GETS BUSY 57

18 FORCED TO PLAY 58

19 REVENGE 60

20 DENTISTS 65

21 COUNTING DOWN THE DAYS 68

22 CHOCOLATES 69

23 LAST ATTACKS FOR NOW 73

24 A STERN WARNING 74

25 WHAT'S WRONG DADDY? 75

26 CALL FOR HELP 78

27 UNCLE BARRY'S COMING 79

28 AUNT JANE'S ARRIVAL 83

29 THE FAMILY NEXT DOOR 86

30 A FORMAL INTRODUC TION 87

31 DAD APPEARS 89

32 NEW CLOTHES & NASTY NIPS 90

33 UNCLE BARRY ARRIVES 93

34 GIFTS GALORE 98

35 MARKET AND BUMPS 100

36 MUM AND AUNT JANE 107

37 GETTING READY FOR ITALY 109

38 GRAN AND POP 111

39 DOVER TO CALAIS 115

40 CIGARETTE BURNS 119

41 WE ARRIVED IN TARANTO	122
42 PIZZA PARLOUR	124
43 HOMEWARD BOUND	135
44 AUNT JANE LEAVES	138
45 NORMAN	140
46 NORMAN'S HOT BATH	143
47 NORMAN DIES	147
48 TWISTED	150
49 LIFE GOES ON	154
50 OPERA AND THE CINEMA	156
51 ABDUCTION	160
52 FRIDAY THE THIRTEENTH	169
53 POP DIES	173
54 MARK'S COMEUPPANCES	178
55 NEW FAMILY	182
56 SCHOOL FIGHT	184
57 COTTON	189
58 JENNY AND DAD	191
59 MARRIAGE ADVICE	197
60 BLUE PAINT	202
61 BROTHER'S 18th BIRTHDAY	206
62 WHITE PLASTIC BAGS	216
63 BACK TO COLLECT	218
64 THE LIVING ROOM	221

65 DINING ROOM	223
66 THE BATHROOM	225
67 PARENT'S ROOM	228
68 FRED'S IN THE HOTHOUSE	230

Warning

Bully contains graphic scenes of violence, an abduction, toned down lewdness, and strong profanities, (which have been reduced).

This book is not intended to offend anyone.

Disclaimer

Names, locations, and several identifying factors have been changed to protect the privacy of those alive and those who have passed.

This Memoir is a compilation of memories I have as a child. The dialogue is true, but not verbatim, the timelines are not completely accurate. I have pieced my memories together to the best of my ability.

Copyright

All rights reserved. No part/s of this book may be scanned, reproduced, or distributed in any printed, copied, form, audio, or other, without written permission. Purchase to be made through authorized editions.

Cover design/book Copyright © 2018 by Hattie Thompson.

Dedications

To those I love and those I have lost, this book is for you.

1 BUCKLED LEGS

My legs buckled as my entire body trembled with fear. I glared down at my shaking knee caps demanding they stop and remain still as my head throbbed from an overload of confusing emotions and questions; I needed answering. I could feel my tummy join in with the anxiety as if a ton of bricks had dropped to its pit, as my pounding heart seemed ready to burst through my beautiful new yellow dress. Hot bile scorched my throat and tears that wouldn't fall stung my eyes.

I was almost eight years old and there was an evil event occurring beyond the door which I didn't dare open.

Someone was in our living room, causing a terrible racket.

It was difficult trying to control my erratic breathing and not move or make a sound because I believed if the people in there heard me, out here, they would come for me. I dreaded what might happen; I feared for my life.

The television blared out insanely. Seconds later, the shrill screaming started, I didn't know which was loudest. Next came a short, silent pause, followed by loud wailing, which ripped through my soul.

I heard two voices but recognised neither. One person's voice sounded stifled and terrified, that must have been from the person who screamed, the other; aggressive and intimidating. It seemed certain whoever it was in there, was here to kill us, it sounded like the killing had already begun!

2 THEY'RE NOT STEALING

My young mind flipped somersaults as I tried to calm down and figure out who the people in the living room could be. Child's logic told me they weren't thieves because we had nothing a thief would want. I knew our belongings were scruffy, old, and fit for the bin as I'd had my face rubbed in that fact by my cousin Katie who's one month younger than me, who took it upon herself to make our impoverishment perfectly clear during a recent visit to her family home.

As I stood petrified, and confused by the door, my mind involuntarily distracted me from what was happening in our house. Amongst other things, I recalled that dreadful visit to my cousin's house...

The previous Saturday Dad ordered my brother Michael and me out of the house, using a voice that sounded angry and a manner that seemed impatient, saying we needed to visit our cousins; he'd already phoned Aunt Sarah to let her know we were on our way. Neither Michael nor I wanted to go, but Dad said; *"You're both bloody well going, or else!"* We didn't know what or else meant; it didn't sound good, so we grabbed our coats and left.

Michael and I walked seven miles to our cousin's new house, stopping on route to pick crab apples and blackberries. We'd almost arrived at our cousin's house when Michael giggled and said; "See you later Hattie." He'd spotted cousin Paul halfway down the road, running to greet us. They disappeared into the woods nearby as I continued walking to the house to play with Katie. I didn't have a clue what to say about Michael running off with Paul.

There was a pond in the woods, full of frogs. Michael had brought a net and a bucket to catch a few. If Aunt Sarah knew Michael had sneaked off to fish and taken Paul with him, she would be furious, as the pond was more of a smelly quagmire and Paul would end up filthy.

Aunt Sarah didn't like her children getting messy or playing in the fresh air, we couldn't understand why not, as we loved it. Mum didn't mind us going home muddy as long as we'd enjoyed ourselves, she said children need to have fresh air, fun, and run off excess energy as it helps with sleep, appetite, and the mind, and dirty clothes were no big deal, as they could be cleaned.

I walked up Katie's path and knocked on the fancy lion-headed knocker on the varnished front door. Aunt Sarah opened the door for me, and I reluctantly entered their beautiful house. It was immaculate inside as if it was still up for sale.

Aunt Sarah ushered me into the hallway and through to the lounge. She didn't speak once, not even to say *hello*, only pointed for me to sit on the white leather sofa covered with a plastic sheet to protect it from filth. I wondered if they put it on only when we visited.

It was uncomfortable sitting on the plastic sheeting and I instantly regretted not having run off with Michael and Paul who were great fun, whereas Katie was boring, she would no doubt irritate and annoy me, as she had most times, I saw her, recently.

Ten minutes later, Katie swooped into the room and shoved her face up to mine, then dragged me by my sleeve to her bedroom, where she motioned for me to sit on the corner of her bed, using the same hand signals and attitude as her bossy mother.

As I sat down, she introduced her dolls, in a squeaky voice, and pushed them into my face. Noting I was irritated and bored, she threw the lovely dolls across the room, then danced ballerina style, leaping towards her wardrobes.

"I'll bet ya've nothing like this little lot I'm gonna show yar, Hattie Thompson," Katie sneered at me in her expensive accent, which she struggled to master; as I tried to stifle a giggle. "What does ya've and yar mean," I asked a tad sarcastically. She looked furious and ignored my question.

Katie and Paul attended elocution lessons each week, in an attempt to change their dialect. Both had been having self-improvement classes since Aunt Sarah's recent huge win on the pools. I felt a little guilty for mocking my cousin, but I was furious at her for having become such a snobby show-off. Two months ago, she lived on the same council estate as us and wore my hand-me-downs. Katie had been different then, she'd been nice.

Mum told us money changes people and too much makes them assume superiority over others. That fact was true, it happened to Katie, Aunt Sarah, and Uncle Ernie, Paul so far, had kept his natural character. Dad said Uncle Ernie thought himself now too posh to acknowledge anyone who didn't drive a brand-new car. Gran said it was; "Empty swank," and that Aunt Sarah had always thought herself a cut above the rest of us, just because she came second in a beauty pageant.

Katie opened the doors to her fitted wardrobes which housed many expensive clothes, all lined up and arranged by colour on cloth, wrapped hangers. She looked me up and down in disgust and said; "You are so scruffy Hattie Thompson." Feeling myself rise, I said. "You're right Katie, I am scruffy, you were too."

"Well, I'm not anymore, but you still are," she snarled.

"Well, we didn't win the pools did we? And another thing, you're nasty and I'm only here because my dad forced me to come." I snarled back.

"Well Hattie Thompson, I'm not interested in all that. I demand an answer. Do you have one pretty dress like mine, do yar? I expect yar blooming well don't. Ya've got nothing nice!" she jeered, then spun several times clumsily on pointe. I told her a few more home truths, but she wasn't listening. She continued ballet dancing, and even worse, started singing to drown out my words.

Katie yanked more clothes down from their hangers, wrapped them around herself and continued her dance in front of the mirrors. Remaining seated I watched her comical performance in disbelief as she pushed several items into my face and sang; "Hattie Thompson, put your scruffy clothes into the bin." It was obvious she wanted to play a nasty game that I didn't want to take part in. All I wanted was to leave and join Michael and Paul and have fun.

Katie reminded me of Bette Davis in the movie Baby Jane, not only the way she looked but how she acted. Michael and I had sneaked downstairs to watch it last week after Mum and Dad went to bed. The sight of the scary lady horrified me and the wicked things she did to her sister shocked me, but the comparison humoured me as I struggled to contain my belly laughter.

Mum often told me to control my giggles. She said things I found funny might not be funny to others, but I saw humour where it didn't seem to exist to anyone else. Mum said; "It might be nerves."

"It might just be hilarious," Michael said in my defence. I'd settled for both explanations and soon learned that many people didn't have a sense of humour which was sad as I loved laughing and playing practical jokes. Michael did too.

Katie looked tense as I remained seated. I hoped she'd tire soon so I could leave and join the boys, but she was up to something. My curiosity forced me to wait to find out what else she had to say.

Katie stopped dancing, looked at me then began; "Hattie my mummy sez yar lot are all poor, is it true, is it, is it? Are yar lot poor, are yar, are yar?" Her haughty face and attitude seemed desperate as she demanded an answer. Her elocution lessons confused her speech pattern. Her facial expressions looked almost demonic, as she waited for my reply to her insulting question, it seemed she needed confirmation that her mother's words were true. Rather than argue, correct her pronunciation, or get angry, I gazed at her, watching her body language become superior. She seemed to have grown an extra inch as she held her head up high, whilst looking down her nose at me. Letting her feel powerful, I confessed; "Yes Katie, *us lot* are poor." Glancing upwards, I caught her expression; it was as I expected, smug, triumphant, and annoying.

Then I let her have it; "We might be poor, but I'm not a nasty, show off like you Katie Gregory; Oh, and another thing, a pools win doesn't give you the right to be a bitch," I added wiping the smile off her face, then stood next to her, towering over her with a scowl on my face.

"Mummy, Mummy," she yelled, becoming hysterical. I'd hit a raw nerve; she ran off mortified. I called after her in my snootiest accent; "Don't give it, if you can't take it! Katie Gregory." Then fell backwards, on the bed, giggling.

Aunt Sarah, came storming in, wagging her finger, yelling fifty words to the dozen, aiming her disgust at me, banning me from the house. She yanked me off the bed. Her hand grabbed me by the scruff of my neck and she frog-marched me towards the front door. I told her to ask Katie how she'd insulted me, to find out what happened, thinking my suggestion reasonable. She thought it was insolent. "Little girls should be seen and not heard Hattie Thompson. You've always got a comeback, haven't you?" she screeched, furiously. She was right, I often had a comeback, Mum had told me to stick up for myself and that older people are not always in the right. I knew Aunt Sarah was in the wrong, and that she'd lost control of the situation because she was yelling as hysterically as Katie. Mum had also told us that when an adult screams and yells, then they've 'lost it,' and that talking things through civilly was the right way for both children and adults to sort things out.

"You should tell that to Katie, she's rude." I screeched back, mirroring her.

Suddenly I felt her hand shove hard into my back as she pushed me through the door and off the step. "Oh go away and don't come back. Go on, get out. You're a cheeky little madam," she snarled, trying to keep her voice down so the neighbours wouldn't hear.

"One day you'll see what a spoiled brat she is, then you'll realise you treated me badly. And another thing, my mum says you don't hurt children, and you've shoved me off the step, that's an assault!" I shouted as loud as I could, so the neighbours *would hear*. She didn't want to listen to another word, so slammed the door shut in my face. Mum would be proud I'd stood up for myself.

My aunt was as rude as Katie. I'd tell Mum what happened when I got home before Aunt Sarah got in first with her version, which I doubted would be the true one.

As I made my way along the road, towards the woods, I spotted Michael playing with Paul, who looked so much happier than he had when we arrived. He was now filthy and soaking wet having enjoyed himself. "We caught eight newts, two frogs, and lots of tadpoles," he boasted, his face beaming.

"That's great Paul, well done, now show them to Katie and your mummy and ask Katie to put them back in the pond," I said, smiling. Aunt Sarah and Katie would scream like mad when they looked inside the bucket.

Paul ran towards the spotless house in his muddy Wellington boots carrying Michael's bucket full of green, smelly pond water and slimy critters.

As Michael and I headed back to our house. I told him; "I'm banned," he threw his head back laughing, and said, "Well done."

We arrived home and saw Mum in the garden. She looked as if she'd been crying, but brightened upon seeing us. I told her what happened, she said; "Hmm, it seems their pool's win has gone to their heads. I'm not surprised. Hattie, I know we don't have much but we should be thankful as some people have even less."

"I know Mum, I am thankful," I said, giving her a long hug. She hugged me back, I was sure I felt her body tremble.

Katie's words struck home; she'd said we were poor; I didn't know if that was true. What I did know, was that whatever we had wasn't worth stealing, Katie had confirmed it because that's what her mother told her. So, who was it inside our house making such a racket? What did they want if it wasn't to steal from us?

3 MICHAEL'S MUSIC LESSONS

Petrified with my eyes closed tight and my ear pressed hard against the door awful thoughts overwhelmed me, placing my mind into a state of absolute chaos.

The telepathic messages I tried to send to Michael, begging him to return home had no effect. He needed to be with me as this was too much for me to face alone.

If Michael saw me standing by this door, looking so pathetic, he'd ask; "What's up Hattie, why are you standing there like a coward?" He'd grab my hand, and we'd barge through that door, he'd know what to do, but he left a short time ago and wasn't due back for hours.

Michael had advanced music lessons on the other side of town, the school funded his frequent return taxi rides. He was rehearsing for a concert that's coming up in two days. Advertising posters had been put up everywhere. I was glad my brother was somewhere else, far from the chaos taking place in our living room. Michael would be safer with his teachers and pupils, oblivious to what was happening here.

It was thanks to Mr. Evans, Michael's headmaster, that he received special classes for skilled and talented children. Soon after Michael started junior school, Mr. Evans requested Mum and Dad's presence; to discuss something of importance, both were clueless about what it could be, but the headmaster had summoned them, so they had to go. I begged to tag along as I didn't want to miss out on anything.

We waited outside the headmaster's office, having arrived early, hoping nothing was wrong. A petite lady popped her head out of the office door; "Mr. and Mrs. Thompson, children, please come in," she beckoned. "Mr. Evans will be here in a moment."

Scurrying in, we suddenly stood to attention; I don't know why, but we all looked guilty.

Mr. Evans entered the room. He was a happy-looking man, dressed in a smart suit with a perfect knot in his tie. His eyes sparkled, and he bore a massive grin, so wide he struggled to open his mouth wide enough to speak. We felt relieved once we realised nothing was wrong. Mr. Evans grinned at Michael; I thought his face must be aching. He shook hands with us, with a wonderful strong grip. Mum had told us you can learn about a person by their handshake and I liked his, and him, we all did.

"We believe Michael is a child prodigy. He's extremely gifted, and with our training and full support Michael could very easily become a superb musician," he boasted, nodding his head, affirming each word. "Michael told me he'd never played the trumpet before, yet he picked it up and played straight away, joining in with one of the big bands I played for him on the record player. He's amazing, with an excellent ear for music. I've spoken with the music department and we all want to do everything possible to further his remarkable talent. If you agree, we would like to send him to music classes for gifted children."

I stood next to Michael squealing proudly, as my head wobbled, every time Michael received a compliment, finding myself caught up in the headmaster's excitement.

Michael kept nudging me with his elbow; "Stop it, you look silly Hattie," he whispered, but I found it impossible to stop. I was happy for him and proud he had a talent. Mum was over the moon too, she became speechless, as tears of pride filled her eyes.

Mr. Evans handed Mum and Dad papers to sign to grant permission for Michael to attend classes, at various Academies in the city. They read the papers and signed them in their best copperplate signatures. Mum looked so proud, but Dad's facial expressions looked strange. I'd never seen him like that before. Mr. Evans said; "I have good vibes about Michael, he may become a famous musician one day, let's just wait and see." That's when Dad stormed out.

Dad never told us why he'd left the meeting so rudely, he should have stayed. It seemed that he was jealous of the praise Michael received, as that evening I heard Dad say to Mum; "You think the sun shines out of Michael's arse." His words horrified me. It was impossible to understand his nastiness after hearing good news about his son's talent which should have been cause for celebration.

4 WHY I'M STOOD BY THE DOOR

Michael progressed with his school subjects and was making a good name for himself with music, sports, and as a scholar. Mr. Evans was so pleased with Michael that he gave me a French horn to learn soon after I started attending the same school, without testing my ability.

"Hattie, it's your turn now," Mr. Evans announced, expecting me to follow in Michael's footsteps, assuming that as we were similar in most things, then I would be an excellent, natural musician too, but he was wrong, I was anything but.

Mum had grave doubts when she saw me arrive home from school, lugging the huge instrument, looking sad and flustered. "I think it's going to be a lot of hard work for you, Hattie," she said knowing I had no interest in music. This was daunting to me and not what I wanted, it felt like a punishment rather than an opportunity, and I had tried to warn Mr. Evans that I didn't want to play it. I'd felt sick when he removed the intricate instrument from its case to show me. Mr. Evans had been so enthusiastic, but I wasn't. I was overwhelmed by the magnificence and complexity of it all, yet I walked away with it, promising to try my best as I stifled my tears, knowing I stood no chance.

The headmaster's kindness caused me no end of trouble; it's the reason I'm not at school today and why I'm standing by this door, all because of another jealous person, a girl in my class.

After months of gruelling practice, I struggled to play a single tune and was fed up dragging the huge cased instrument between home and school, along with my books and sports bag. The weight and awkwardness slowed me down as I made my way along the frightening tarmacked path, which I had to take, bordered with overgrown trees, bushes, and derelict buildings. I'd run down that horrid path as fast as my legs would carry me, relieved to have reached its end. It wasn't safe there. The kids at school told me that naughty men hid along that path, "flashers," they called them, but I didn't know what that meant, not until Jamie Morris told me in gory detail, needless to say, I was horrified. These flashers would leap out from the bushes and scare children that walked alone. It wasn't a lie; the police came around to school to warn us, during assembly. They mentioned robbers as well. So far no one had been caught. This knowledge worried me as I had to take that route, slowed down by my extra baggage, but I had no choice. I couldn't return the bulky, instrument, not yet, I needed to keep practicing and carry it to and from school, until Mr. Evans told me to stop.

My lack of progress and enthusiasm with the horn affected Sally James. It seemed she wanted it and had been watching me ever since I'd walked out of the storeroom with Mr. Evans. I'd hoped her envy would pass, but it escalated into a toxic obsession where she'd say nasty things and threaten me, every time she saw me.

Sally had convinced herself that I'd stolen her golden opportunity of playing the horn, though she struggled with the recorder, it was unlikely she would have been chosen in the first place. I knew if it hadn't been for Michael's gift for music, neither would I.

Now I have an instrument I can't play which I carry as a burden along the dreaded path, and I'm being punished by Sally's constant bitching. My temper was fraying but I kept quiet, hoping she'd stop bothering me. It was a lot for me to deal with and some days I dreaded going to school because of her.

Sally hung around with a gang of older kids after school, loitering by the off-license, smoking, drinking cider, and swearing, all to gain some kind of attention, we'd all seen her. She was ten years old, the oldest girl in our class, I was the youngest. I tried avoiding her, but she seemed intent on seeking me out to harass me. At break times

Sally walked the school playground and corridors in a gang, made up of kids whom she'd bullied into joining, or others who enjoyed bullying as much as she did. On mass, they were intimidating, and many kids were scared of her and her gang, alone, they were cowards.

Sally cornered me during break- time a few days ago, as I walked along the corridor. She grabbed me by my hair then started ranting on and on over the horn. I said; "Come on Sally, we'll tell Mr. Evans how unfair you think it is. You can tell him you'll be much better at playing it than me and that I want you to have it. You can even ask him why he gave it to me, and not to you. Come on, Sally, let's go." Sally said nothing, only pulled my hair harder, becoming angrier. She hadn't expected me to speak, but I was a talker, I couldn't stop and I thought I was being reasonable. She called me a *big-mouthed bitch* and refused to budge, still gripping my hair. I wanted to fight her off, but thought better of it, her reputation bothered me. It was possible I might lose. I asked her; "What's wrong, don't you want it now?" She stared at me with cold steely eyes and said nothing.

"Are you too scared to tell him?" I asked, becoming riled. She didn't answer. I could tell she was seething, as her face became mobile, her nose twitched, as she sank her top teeth into her bottom lip. Sally gave my hair one final hard yank then let go, as Mr. Davis, a substitute teacher walked by tutting. She didn't want any trouble with him, neither did I. He was renowned for throwing blackboard dusters, aimed at the pupil's heads, and clouting any kid in his path across the ear. I hoped he would never teach me, but at that moment I was glad he'd walked past.

"I'll knock the shit out of you Hattie Thompson, you talk too much," she hissed. Feeling myself getting angrier. I took a quick look round to ensure Mr. Davis had gone. "Go on then, try it, or are you too chicken for that as well?" I asked, stepping into her body space, looking confident, but regretting I had reacted to her threat so cockily. "One day, I'll make you pay Hattie Thompson; it should be me on the French horn," she screeched. Mirroring her voice, I screeched back; "You'll be crap on it like you are on the recorder!"

Sally stormed off, cursing, making more dreadful threats, which I knew she would follow through with, I just didn't know when. I thought it would be today, that's why I didn't go to school and pretended I was sick.

It turned out I was needed more at home where the commotion is getting worse.

Memories of Mark Willis filled my troubled mind, overtaking those of Sally. I'd never met nasty people like these two before, thankfully Mum had warned me that nasty people do exist, so I wasn't totally surprised. I remembered Mum's words before my starting school; "It doesn't matter how nice or well behaved you are Hattie, it doesn't mean everyone will like you, people can get jealous and nasty for reasons unbeknown to you. If someone upsets you, tell me, but you must try to deal with it yourself, that's how you grow up." Her words of wisdom were to prepare me for what is turning into a frightening world. I didn't understand how bad it would get; I was finding out, albeit too quickly.

5 MARK WILLIS FLASHBACK

Sally's hostility toward me had started only weeks after I started school. I also noticed Mark Willis spying on me but had no idea he'd wanted to hurt me. It was possible Sally's vendetta against me had triggered him.

Mum and Dad had told Michael and me; "Boys shouldn't hit girls, anyone weaker, smaller, or wearing glasses." This teaching gave me a false sense of security, as I was to find out, it wasn't a rule that everyone followed, especially Mark Willis.

Mark Willis lived two doors up from our house, he had an aura about him that made every hair on my body stand on end. I remembered Mum's warning; "Trust your gut instincts, Hattie, as I told you before many times, we don't know who is good or who is bad." My gut instincts warned me he was dangerous and not one of the good types, sadly my instincts didn't save me.

It was dark by the time school ended on that dreadful afternoon in mid-January; I was desperate to get home. The overgrown path I had to take spooked me even more now I knew flashers hid along there waiting for victims. I became anxious as I began my journey home. My imagination ran riot as I scanned every bush and shadow, trying to look everywhere, as I tottered onward, skidding on icy patches every few paces, lugging my French horn in one cold hand, my sports bag in the other, a satchel of books and a lumpy pencil case strapped to my back.

It had snowed throughout the day, now it was hail stoning and blowing a furious gale; I was tired, freezing and hard hailstones battered my face, causing me to keep blinking to keep the elements out of my eyes.

I'd left school through the back gate, as I usually did, everyone else who used the same route had long since passed by, there was only me on the path as far as I knew.

All of a sudden, I got ambushed, by Mark Willis. He must have lain in wait for some time, hiding in the bushes; he pounced on me, screeching incoherent garbage, looking bonkers, as he jumped up and down in front of me, then he pushed me down hard with both hands, causing me to land flat onto my satchel, hurting my spine as I landed on the bumpy path. The heavy case fell on me slamming hard against my face, my vision blurred as my eyes smarted. Terrified, I screamed for help.

Mark got started; he dropped on top of me, belly down, deadweight style, winding me, then he became delirious as he stuffed handfuls of snow into my mouth which stopped my screams. He shoved snow down my clothes and vest with his rough, bony hands, as I thrashed my head from one side to the other, trying to avoid being suffocated with cold, dirty snowballs mixed with grit from the tarmacked path which I struggled to spit back out.

I had no chance to fight back as I couldn't get up. He'd successfully prevented me from doing anything, and Mr. Evans had given me strict instructions to protect the instrument at all costs; that was my main worry. "You'll have to pay for any repairs if you break it," warned Mr. Evans when he'd handed it over. Mum said a French Horn would cost a fortune to repair. We had no money to pay for repairs, so I guarded it with my life and took the beating in the hope Mark Willis wouldn't damage it.

Mark lay on top of me for ages, pondering his next moves; he'd become disturbed, and controlling, feeding on the power he had over me. The element of surprise had enabled his frenzied attack. His exhilarated smug face knocked me sick. At last, he'd caught me;

his stalking had paid off. I wondered if he was one of the flashers that hung down this path; it seemed likely.

Mark was almost three years older than me, way taller, it seemed he needed to teach me a lesson; I didn't know why, I'd never spoken to him, perhaps that was his problem.

It was impossible for me to fight him off or even move; he found that amusing and became hysterical, as he continued stuffing snow into my mouth and all over my face, rubbing it in as hard as he could until my face became raw and my eyes smarted so much that I couldn't see. Spitting the snow out, I screamed in agony, fear, and rage. I swore he would not get away with this. If he ever tried it again, I'd be ready, and I'd give him a taste of his own medicine.

Mark Willis decided he'd done enough damage and smacked my face hard several times, stinging my cheeks as a finale, after which he ran off like a thief into the night.

With my sight-impaired, I gathered my belongings to continue my slow journey home, worried others may be lurking behind the bushes. My vision blurred, my body shaking, the French Horn in one piece, I began my walk home alone, as tears flooded onto my raw, burning cheeks.

Suddenly, the horrible memories of Mark Willis vanished. I'm back to reality, stood by the door, petrified and disturbed as I heard more loud screams which took me from one violent attack and put me straight into another.

A loud crash, more piercing screams which could raise the dead shocked me to the core, as I wet myself in fright. Warm urine soaked my legs and fallen down new lemon socks.

My sticky, stinking wet legs marched on the spot, involuntarily, going nowhere. Overwhelmed with panic, I repeated to no one, the word *help*!

6 MORNING SUNSHINE

A short time ago, Mum had come into my bedroom full of joy; "Good morning Hattie," she'd sung, delighted to see me. I'd smiled back half-heartedly, pretending to be sick. She'd been so bright and cheerful as she gave me a raspberry kiss on my forehead and tweaked my round cheeks; everyone loved my cheeks, likened to plump rosy apples. Everyone wanted to squeeze them. Gran called me; Happy Hattie Apple Cheeks ever since I was small, because I always smiled, making my cheeks plump up. Michael called me *Hamster Face*, which always made me laugh.

Opening my bright yellow curtains to let in the sunshine, Mum said; "Today is a new beautiful sunny day Hattie, so come on, up you get to enjoy it." She was happy to be alive and grateful for each day. Time was precious to Mum, as were Michael and myself, she adored us.

Mum frowned when she noticed my half-hearted smile; "What's wrong Hattie?" she asked. "I'm not feeling very well Mum," I lied, crossing my fingers under the bedclothes to counteract my fib. I didn't like telling fibs or acting like a coward, but this time I believed it to be necessary. Mum believed me and let me stay off school, hoping I'd feel better the next day, then she sat with me until I pretended to fall back to sleep.

I heard Mum sneak out of my room, only to return a moment later, leaving a parcel on my bed

Mum still fumed over Mark Willis's sneaky, attack, she'd raced to his house to tell him off for being a bully and his parents for not keeping a good eye on him. It seemed obvious he hadn't been taught not to hit girls. Even though it happened a while ago, I still hadn't recovered from it. She also knew Sally James had been causing problems for me at school, Michael had told her how she follows me around most days, saying nasty things, but I guessed I had to deal with her so I could grow up a little.

After Mum tiptoed from my room to leave me in peace, curiosity got me out of bed. I wanted to check my beautifully wrapped parcel. I took off the wrapping and saw beneath the sheets of tissue paper lay the prettiest yellow dress and socks I'd ever seen. I tried them on, tying the bow of my pretty dress, but unable to fasten the long zip at the back. My sweet socks looked so pretty. I'd never had brand new clothes before. Emotionally, I twirled around my bedroom, glimpsing my reflection in the tiny heart-shaped mirror of my little wardrobe. It was then, my happy face morphed into a terrified one, on hearing terrible noises coming from the living room, beneath my bedroom. Somehow, I headed towards the commotion, rather than seeking cover under my bedclothes as I normally did at the slightest scary sound. Frightened, I walked towards the noises, hoping the wooden stairs, with carpet patches, nailed down in various patterns and sizes wouldn't creak and draw attention to me on my way down. "Where are you, Mum?" I asked as I continued moving forward, unable to stop nor retreat. Somebody needed me, I had to go, I didn't have a choice, but I continued worrying about her.

Mum was always around the house, so why hadn't she come, to tell me what the banging was all about?

Michael won't think I'm a wimp anymore, I assured myself, feeding myself courage as I begrudgingly placed one foot in front of the other. My legs felt like jelly, and I almost collapsed with fear, yet bravely, I continued forward, sensing today my sunshine would stop shining.

For some reason, I thought Mum must have gone out, and Dad left for work hours ago. Michael left for school around half an hour ago, it seemed there was only me in the house, amidst the violent din, on the other side of the closed living room door.

7 BRAVE AND FEARLESS

Thoughts of Michael continued to flash through my mind, as I dithered over what to do. Even though Michael was only two years older than me, he often gave me big brother advisory lessons. During one of his sessions, he told me the only way not to be scared, was to face fear full-on. To prove his point, he thought up creative ways to terrify me, which he did, too often for my liking. I loved it sometimes, I found him hilarious, and we'd howl with laughter at the pranks he played, but other times he was beyond annoying, pushing me into a state of absolute panic, those times I threatened to tell on him, then he'd call me a snitch or a supergrass which made me feel bad, so I kept quiet.

Michael had an innocent face, even though we looked like twins, my face looked cheekier, full of mischief, and always happy, which somehow made me look like I was fibbing, so Mum didn't always believe me when I told her how Michael scared and tormented me.

Once while Mum and Dad were out Michael turned the electricity off at the mains wanting to give me the fright of my life. He came into the darkened living room and whispered that there was a problem upstairs and that he needed the poker. He left me terrified, huddled on the chair, grasping a cushion for assurance as he sneaked out of the living room, and ran upstairs in the darkness carrying the poker... "Hattie, there are burglars, six of them, he screamed. Then the banging and yelling started. Hysterical, and shaking all over, I tried my best to phone the police.

As the operator answered my call and asked me which emergency service I require, Michael suddenly reappeared by my side and quickly disconnected the call so I couldn't tell them what was going on. "Don't worry Hattie, the burglars have gone now. I sorted all six out," he told me bravely. At that moment he became my hero.

Later I found out he'd set me up. He'd beaten the mattress, not six burglars. I told Mum what he did, to get him into the trouble he deserved, for terrifying me. Yet again, I was smiling, so Mum didn't take me seriously. She said, "Oh Hattie, he's your brother. He's left in charge when we go out because he's responsible, I really don't think he did that." Then tutted at me for being a tell-tale, as Michael smirked, hidden from her view, pulling faces at me, trying to make me laugh.

"No, never, he wouldn't do that," she repeated convinced of his innocence.

"You're wrong, he did do that," I argued, knowing it was pointless. Michael followed me around later, calling me a super-grass and a snitch. I told him he was crap and asked him; "Why are you always scaring me?"

"I'm doing you a favour, I'm training you to be brave and fearless. You may need this training one day," he justified. His explanation somehow made sense, and I believed him, that might be the reason I'm stood by the door, biding my time, because he made me brave and fearless.

8 THE ONLY HELP

Stay with it, Hattie, stop daydreaming, listen, be strong and calm, I told myself as the screams and bangs continued. I don't know how long I stood there for, it must have been for quite some time, as my mind flitted through every memory I could recall during my short life.

It all fell silent for a moment, as an overwhelming eeriness seeped through the gap at the bottom of the door. I heard more painful screeching build to a crescendo, causing every hair on my body to stand on end, it was then I realised the cries of pain and immense suffering were coming from Mum.

"Mum, I'm here," I whispered. She needed me. *What do I do, what do I do?"*

The simmering urge to barge into the living room was building up inside me, but fear had ravaged my entire being, rendering me useless. Remembering the words Michael used to justify tormenting me; *brave and fearless* became paramount within my thoughts. I couldn't let his scare tactics go to waste; he'd trained me for this moment, even though he hadn't known it.

The side of my face was soaking wet from my sweat and tears. My chubby apple cheeks were stuck to the panel of the door as I tried to listen to what was happening. My body stressed, as my muscles flickered with fear, outweighing anything that Michael had ever put me through.

Please, someone, help us, I begged though I knew no one would come. There was only me. I was the only help we had and Mum was on the other side of the door screaming.

9 ACT NOW

I loved my mum, and if I died doing so, I was going through that door to save her. I heard another loud crash, a piercing scream, followed by another devastating wounded moan, it was then that my adrenaline kicked in and took over me. Instantaneously I sprang into action, out of my zombie-like state, drawing on my inner strength and energy.

Recognising the urgent need to save her, I knew if I didn't act immediately, it might be too late. This was a fight or flee situation, I took the fight mode. Even though I was a child, I had to do something; it was impossible not to. So much depended on me. Mum's survival was paramount. I was going in.

My mind cleared of all thoughts, ramblings, and wishes as my instincts took over, though I was terrified. I couldn't wish this away; my whole being told me to act. Bravely I stormed through the door, immediately my adrenaline took a knock backwards, stopping me dead in my tracks, as I took in what I saw and whom. It was Mum being brutalised.

I took another step forward, then froze...

10 THE BULLY REVEALED

Dad, no, no, stop it, stop it!" I screamed. It was Dad, my dad. This was beyond belief. I watched, bewildered, as his fists jabbed at Mum as if she were a punching bag. She slithered down the wall as he towered over her, rendering her helpless. He struck from above with a gusto which told me he enjoyed what he was doing. Pleasure plastered on his face, pure misery and pain on Mums.

Dad saw me as I stood transfixed, my mouth open in shock, and disbelief, he didn't seem to care that I was there, watching. He didn't stop, instead; he picked up the pace, fuelled by my presence. His face displayed a perverse smile on a mouth I wanted to punch.

Dad shouted and muttered words I'd never heard, in a voice that sounded nothing like his. He egged himself on, deeper into his brutal frenzy, going all out to hurt her, maybe even kill her. He'd changed almost beyond recognition, looking demonic. His Adrenaline pumped so much his eyes bulged from their sockets. Obscenities spewed from his mouth along with frothy saliva which dribbled down his chin as he attempted to suck it back in, making a disgusting slurping noise. I'd never observed such vileness, not even at school.

As I stood frozen, watching the horrors unfold before my eyes, I realised I hadn't stopped screaming since I'd walked in on this madness. My heart broke when I looked at Mum, trapped, motionless, and broken. Panic and despair had replaced the happy, face of my mum, who minutes ago came into my room singing and talking about sunshine. Mum was my sunshine. She'd tried to make me smile, as I convinced her I felt too sick to go to school. Now I'm screaming as I watch her being pulverised by Dad, who'd promised to love her till death do they part.

Mum was slumped between the television and the fireplace. The fireguard and poker had been flung across the room. I saw long ash marks on her bare arms. Unable to move towards her, I stepped around the perimeter, unsure of what to do to stop him and help her.

I was a kid, struggling with other kids and what I was witnessing now seemed the same as Mark Willis's assault on me, the only difference being; we were younger and smaller.

Mum screamed as Dad grotesquely twisted her head in my direction. It seemed he wanted to strangle her or break her neck. It was then she saw me. Her frantic eyes seemed to plead with me to run and get help.

Mums' bloodied mouth opened and closed, reminding me of the guppies in Michael's fish tank, trying to call out, without a sound, as she gasped for breath. Somehow, seeing me, Mum gained strength and a determination to retaliate harder. It seemed she'd almost given up fighting for her own survival but now she fought back for me, for Michael, for us, with a new burst of energy.

Mum somehow sensed a split-second opportunity. Dad's legs were apart as he towered over her, she brought her knee up hard and fast, into his privates, as Gran called them. His legs collapsed, he released the stranglehold on Mum, as he tended to his agonised groin. I pumped the air in triumph. Dad had taught us that move, he told us that place hurt men the most. "Ha," I said amidst my tears and screams, I felt almost joyous as I watched him grimace and crumble in pain.

Dad recovered; and punched Mum in the side of her face, wilder and faster, as if punishing her for trying to protect herself. "You don't do that," he spluttered, slavering down his chin, and onto his arm, as he bounced on tiptoes, his fists punching the air, then back towards Mum holding nothing back, striking her face and body. I wished she had kicked him nonstop in his groin until he lay, defeated, and crying, like Mum, as I continued screaming.

11 FIGHTING INSTRUCTIONS

Dad had instructed both Michael and me how to defend and protect ourselves from a young age, almost to a point of obsession. We'd learned various techniques, dreading the day that we may need to use the knowledge he'd drummed into us through role-play and constant practice... "I'm warning both of you; be prepared at all times. Someone will come after you at some stage in your lives, believe me. There are bloody troublemakers everywhere. If a naughty man comes at you, knee him right between the legs, hard and I mean bloody hard!" he said.

"What will he come to us for, and what if it's a lady?" we asked in unison.

"Well, sadly, you can't rule ladies out. You need to be ready for both, they can be rude as well, and want to hurt little kids. Use the techniques I'm teaching you, but only if you have to. If you can run away, then that should be your first option. If you have to fight, then do what I tell you and do it as hard as you bloody well can."

I hadn't realised we needed all this training. I never thought people in the world were this bad. When I told Dad this, he said; "Some people are very good, but others... well..." he paused, then told us about the murderers in the news; a man and woman who had killed lots of children and buried them in the hills never to be found. Dad skipped the grizzly details. It was dreadful, even more so now I'm watching Dad attacking Mum.

When I'm ready, I knew I'd have to use his training against him. He's one of the bloody troublemakers, a terrible one and I can't let him get away with it, that would be wrong. I can't run away, as he's hurting Mum. She needs my help.

Agony and fear were written all over Mum's beautiful face, it didn't look like her anymore, I couldn't understand why he wanted to make her look like that. "Oh Mum, Mum." I mouthed to her. Her sparkle for life and love had gone, it was there an hour ago when she was in my bedroom.

Dad was trying to knock everything happy and beautiful out of her, determined to replace it with fear, pain, and anguish. I could see now; how bad he was, and I'd never get those images out of my head, nor would I forgive or forget, this was unforgivable.

12 IT'S TIME TO FIGHT

"Let go of Mum!" I screamed at Dad, over and over as I found myself standing in the middle of Hell. Everything was happening in quick time, yet somehow in slow motion- "Mum, I'm here, Hattie's here, I promise I will help you," I mouthed. Then I pounced... having snapped out of my trance-like state. The first thing I did, now my Adrenaline and courage had kicked in overriding my fear was jump up on Dad's back. I needed to pull him away from Mum.

I climbed up his legs, using his clothing to pull my way up, pushing my feet into his hips. It was difficult as my new yellow dress was getting in the way. My socks were too slippery to get a good grip. Dad kept bobbing, but I got high enough to grab his hair. My intentions were to yank him off my mum by it, but my hands slid off as he had that disgusting smelly cream in, which was to stop dark hair from turning white and keep it from frizzing.

My beautiful dress had fallen down over my shoulders, restricting my movements, yet I gripped his neck and clung on like a limpet. I wasn't sure if I was helping or making things worse but I must have made a difference as Dad screamed at me telling me I was a *bleeding nuisance* and to *bugger off*.

Dad tried to bump me off his back by slamming me against a wall winding me. Miraculously, I remained in place, with no inkling of what to do next, all I knew was; I had to save my mum, but she was worried about me. Every time she tried to move to help me, she got punched. She needed to forget me and concentrate on herself, that was why I was doing this, for her, not me. She looked out of it. "Don't give up Mum, I'm here, I'm here." I kept trying to shout, but my voice had almost gone. I wanted to give her strength and reassurance though my efforts were futile.

Dad pulled his arm back as far as possible. His fist clenched. knuckles protruding. it thrust forward fast and forcefully, aimed at Mum's jaw. I watched as her hands flew to her mouth, blood oozed down her chin and through her fingers as I dangled off Dad's shoulder. My hands slipped from his neck as my body slithered to the floor. I was absolutely frantic with fear.

Dad caught hold of me, and slapped me hard with the back of his large hand, sending me flying, halfway across the room. Somehow, through necessity, I rebounded and ran to Mum who lay motionless on the floor, almost unrecognisable, beaten to a pulp, I thought he'd killed her.

Shockingly, he kicked her. "Only cowards do that." I tried to yell at him as he looked down at his achievement of a bloodied beautiful woman, the one he vowed to love. It was obvious he was proud of himself. The coward had now lost his family.

Dad stopped ranting and raging, turned around to cough, wheeze, and get his breath back. When he turned back around, ready to continue, he saw me standing with my arms outstretched as a barrier to protect Mum.

Our eyes locked, it was like staring at the devil. Mine challenged him to punch me that was the only way he would move me out of his way. I faced him courageously. He didn't scare me, I'd gone beyond that, I needed to save my mum. My fear was for her. If he killed her, then I didn't want to live without her, but what would happen to Michael?

Mum strove to get up, but she was too wounded and weak, there was no fight left in her. She saw me struggling to protect her; I was so lost and bewildered, yet I recognised she was still with me, still alive.

Dad looked like he was about ready to stop his brutal assaults. He looked at me, seeming proud and amused that I was still fighting. I held his stare searching for a soul he no longer had.

I glanced at Mum; she had put up a serious defence. She'd been fighting for her life, long before I'd opened the door and gone into the room. Mum was mentally and physically strong, she must have held her own for quite some time and fought hard. She opened her eyes, after what seemed like hours, bewildered and confused. Her face was swollen with slits showing instead of huge brown eyes. The horror of what Dad had done to her made me sick.

"Someone please help us," I pleaded, knowing no one would come, this might be our end. Dad switched his attention to me. His hands swooped, to grab me. He lifted me high, his face looked amused, as he flung me across the room. He stormed out, snarling, "Fucking little bitch." I found myself flat on my face on the rough nylon rug. My shaking kneecaps had carpet burns, leaving me sobbing from the stinging sensation and pain. I picked myself up, unsure which way to turn, or what to do, hoping Dad would leave us alone now. Looking at Mum, I realised how helpless we were.

Dad clattered around in the bathroom at the top of the stairs. His usual loud vulgar noises started. He pulled the chain. Seconds later, the feeling of dread returned, as he ran down the stairs with new vigour.

He's back, prancing over Mum, jeering, spitting, and slapping her across her face, fast, and hard to liven her up, to cajole her into humouring him by fighting back, with the energy she no longer had. It seemed Dad wanted to watch Mum's weakness against his manic strength. This was a depth of depravity beyond comprehension.

13 THE SHIRT

Dad often said if you pick a fight, it should be with someone your own size. We didn't want to pick fights with anyone, but we would try to defend ourselves if someone picked on us.

I vowed if I survived this, I'd sort Mark Willis out if he picked on me again and I wouldn't hide from Sally James ever again.

Dad's shirt hung over his trousers, as he bent over Mum to torment her further. I remembered Mum saying, 'Len, tuck your shirt in, it makes you look untidy,' that memory was the clue. Now I knew what to do to save her...

Grasping at his hanging shirttails with both hands, I pulled down hard. At first, it seemed impossible to get enough of a grip, as Dad was bending down, but when he felt me tugging, he stood up and tried to thwack me off. Once he was upright, I wrapped the shirt tighter around each hand, at the same time; dodged his efforts to swat me away.

I kept tugging, becoming hyper as I yanked at his shirt, leaning as far back as I could go, trying my best to stop him from inflicting more injuries and pain to my mum, it felt like we were coming to the end of this battle, and he was going for the Kill.

"Hattie, get off me," he yelled as he tried to grab me with one hand whilst the other thrashed out at nothing. He'd lost his momentum, stopped swinging his arms so much, but that wasn't enough, it would only help for a little time. I had to continue using this technique as it was slowing him down, but I needed something else, it wasn't as drastic as I thought it would be, all I was doing was annoying him and stalling for time. It seemed I was too low down, acting as an anchor, I didn't have the weight to drag him over. What I needed to do was climb higher and yank his collar.

Michael seemed to be with me saying; "Calm down Hattie, pull Dad's collar, climb up, and don't stop. Get him off Mum. Save Mum. Good girl, you will save her, get up there and pull him over." Thinking of Michael helped me. I didn't want to let him down.

My annoying presence irritated Dad. He kept trying to slam me off, as I ran up his legs like a ladder in bare feet, my pretty socks had long gone. I had no idea where my dress was, but I had a better grip now.

Taking hold of Dad's collar, I gripped it as hard as possible and pulled him backwards. There was no way I would let go, not until he promised never to hurt Mum again. "Drop down Hattie, don't think about it, just do it," said a voice in my head, again I believed it to be Michaels.

As I dropped dead weight style, I didn't expect the gurgling and horror that came with my move. Dad stumbled backwards; as I tugged hard, possessed by a force I didn't recognise. Dad's huge hands stopped punching, he needed them to save himself.

My small hands were becoming numb in my urgency to incapacitate him as time was running out. I glanced at Mum, wishing for a miracle. Mum caught my gaze and gave me a slight nod. Her expression seemed to say; "Yes Hattie, this is helping me, this will stop him, keep on, good girl." I visualised Michael by Mum's side, nodding with her. I hated doing this, but I had to, otherwise Mum would die at the hands of Dad.

Dad's collar bit into his throat as he wobbled all over the place. His weak state apparent.

The horrible guttural noises he made told me his plan had backfired. Now it was me in control, taking him to the brink, as he wheezed and gagged. "I will save you, Mum, I'm doing this to help you," I tried to scream to let her know, but Mum knew. It was Dad's turn to suffer.

Dad turned to yell at me, which was a bad move, he'd just tightened his own collar. He was at my mercy, but I had none. His fear fed my frenzy, his crime fitted my punishment. Upping my game, I remembered Dad saying, "Take no prisoners," so; I lay flat down, shuffling backwards as I continued tugging at his collar, making him gag and wheeze more.

The entire neighbourhood must have heard the screams, the shattering of glass, and the acts of violence. Yet no one called the police, no one cared. This was entertainment, something to gossip about for the next few weeks until somebody else kicked off.

My teeth ground together, as I mustered every ounce of strength, I had at the same time draining his, using techniques he'd taught me and instincts that came with protectionism and survival. I wasn't only saving Mum; I was also punishing my dad, teaching him a bloody lesson, bullying the bully like he'd told us to do. It was his turn to experience panic and as much pain as I could inflict on him as he did to Mum. I was teaching the bad man a lesson, one which served him bloody well right!

14 UNSTOPPABLE

Dad hadn't realised I was strong enough to put up such an aggressive fight in defence of Mum. He'd shrugged me off as a silly little girl, a damned nuisance, one who should have remained seen and not heard, as he'd concentrated on doing his worse.

My instincts told me to fight with everything I had and save her. This feral child I'd become didn't seem like me. I'd always been cute cuddly Hattie who danced, wrapped in net curtains pretending I was in a wedding dress. This was me now.

Dad had successfully destroyed my childhood, before my eighth birthday. Now I was one of the sad victims I'd heard about and felt bad for. Never would I forgive this man, the one who used to be my dad. The new me was ready to do anything to save Mum. I was at the edge, terrified of the consequences that would occur If I released my pain-inflicting grip, which was affecting him. I was sure he'd kill me if I let go, so I remained with his shirt in my hands, doing my worst, absolutely panic-stricken.

Mum screamed again, but this time at me, to snap me out of my trance; "Hattie, let go, he can't breathe," her voice sounded broken.

'No,' I gestured shaking my head. I hadn't finished yet.

"Hattie, listen to me, you must stop. You're hurting him. He needs his inhaler," Mum said. Her speech had slowed down to emphasise the severity of my actions. She could beg, but it wouldn't change anything. I wasn't stopping yet, only when he did. Mum's frail voice upset me; he had no right to make her voice sound like that. I tugged harder.

Dad's wheezing and choking noises sounded horrible, he reminded me of the donkeys on the beach that ran all day, giving kids like me rides. Dad had overexerted himself; it was his own fault. His friend, Doctor Stevens had warned him, not to overdo things. I wondered what his friend would say if he saw him now, and us. "He's got bronchitis," Doctor Stevens had announced several months ago. We'd all felt sorry for him. I cried when he told us he was sick, but now his condition was helping us.

Mum explained his condition to us and told us what to do if he ever got into difficulty breathing; "Always give him his inhaler, the blue one in the cupboard," she said as Dad stood by her side enjoying the drama, attention, and my sympathetic sobs. Together they showed Michael and me how he should put the inhaler in his mouth, press it, suck it, deep into his lungs, hold it, then blow out. If that didn't work, we had to bang him on the chest, or back, to help him. Should our efforts prove futile, then we had to continue banging on his chest, whilst the other rang for an ambulance.

I'd loved Dad with all my heart and wanted him to be healthy, not sick with bronchitis, and need an inhaler. Now I didn't love him; he'd never receive first aid from me, not after this.

I stopped thinking about the first aid drill, startled to find Mum still shouting at me; "Hattie, stop, that's enough, let go right now!" Mum's voice seemed frantic and weak, it kept breaking off, I ignored her. "Hattie, you must stop, he can't breathe."

"No, he'll kill us. I won't stop, he hates us, and wants us dead." The realisation of what he was doing and what I was doing to stop him, hit me full on. I hyperventilated and slowed down. My hands were numb, swollen, and raw where his shirt had cut into them, the look of them caused me to throw up as I watched his shirt unravel from my exhausted, painful grip.

Dad stumbled. He seemed exhausted and fell to the floor, cursing, whilst rubbing his throat. I retreated, into a corner, tucking myself into a foetal position. Hugging my knees, as I sobbed silently. My tears dry.

I rocked myself to find comfort, there was none. I'd tried my best to save Mum and had succeeded. Now I had to grieve for myself and for us. Shock possessed me. I felt myself shake. I was freezing, moaning, and convulsing as Mum dragged herself beside me, she pulled me to her and rocked me in her loving arms. My painful, bleeding hands touched her face, hands, shoulders, legs, trying to make her better by touch alone. My whole body cringed as I took in the state of her.

Still petrified, I looked at Dad, worried he would start his attacks again. After what seemed like hours, my wracking sobs subsided, my body relaxed, I looked to Mum who was clinging onto me. Pulling her hands off me, I wriggled away, to do one last thing; Dad's glasses lay on the floor, I tottered across the room towards them and picked up the poker, and smashed them to bits, so he would never see us again.

My attention turned to Dad who was down on the floor, as if he was the victim, I raised the poker above my head, as Dad's hands flew to shield himself having recognised my intentions... Just as I was about to whack him full force, Mum removed the poker from my hands, scooped me up into her arms, and took me away.

Staring ahead, lost, and bewildered, she carried me to the bathroom. I felt her wet my face as if trying to bring me back from wherever it was, I'd disappeared to. Her lips moved, but it was impossible to grasp what she was saying. Focusing on her face, I homed in on her bruises, the blood, and her sad, frightened eyes. My thoughts had told me she was dying and yet she'd summoned her last breath to carry me. "Mum, I stopped him," I whispered, battling to tell her with a voice that was barely there.

"I know Hattie, I know, thank you. I'm so sorry you saw this, so, so, sorry, hush now little Hattie." Mum's brokenness was tangible, her tears streamed onto my face as she forced herself to carry me to my little yellow box room, towards peace and recovery. Nestling in her loving arms, I burrowed my head into her armpit, to hide.

Mum placed me on my bed, pulling my old sheet and rough army blankets up to my chin, then sat with me, ignoring her own pain, watching me until I slept.

15 JABS AND THE AFTERMATH

I woke with my legs thrashing and my fists flying, trying to shout out for help as the horrors I'd witnessed came rushing back as if they were happening all over again, one brutal punch after the other. I saw that monster's fist ramming into Mum's lovely face and Dad's twisted one leering at us.

My mattress and pyjamas were soaked, from my sweat and urine, my body felt heavy and sore. I heard the front door open with the turn of a key. A wave of panic swept over me as I worried it was Dad, but It was Michael, returning home from school. He sounded furious. "Where is he? I'll kill him," he shouted, loud enough for me to hear from my room.

I changed into my spare pair of tatty pyjamas and made my way downstairs, flinching and trembling, with shock. I needed my brother. As I stood on the bottom stair, I felt the violent atmosphere still in the air. Dad had gone out, but his evil remained.

Michael was sat on the plastic mustard coloured settee with ragged brown cushions, looking at Mum as she stroked his hair, telling him not to worry, this wouldn't happen again, her voice filled with emotion, she'd sounded so different earlier this morning, when she'd been happy. "We will get over this!" Mum stated, convincing no one. I didn't believe her. Couldn't Mum see this was the start of things to come? It was obvious, we were done for. I watched as Michael scanned the bruises on Mum's face, her ripped clothes, and the dried blood. He listened to how I'd tried so hard to stop the attack. Michael's hands opened and closed with rage.

"Hattie saved me," Mum said overcome with emotion. I looked at her, she should have gone to the hospital, but Mum, wouldn't want anyone to see her in such a state.

Michael had come home early from school, He'd received a booster shot, against diseases and had reacted quite badly. The headmaster cancelled his music lesson and the school secretary rang to ask Mum or Dad to collect him, but no one heard the phone ringing out. He'd had to sit in the sick room until a teacher brought him back to the house. Only for him to walk into the aftermath of a brutal battle.

Michael's sadness was replaced with a determination to end this brutality; "We have to stop him, we have to do something," he said, trying to think of what, but we were too young and too shocked to know what to do. Our thoughts were to call the police, but we knew that would not happen.

Michael took hold of my hand and Mums, he told me he was proud of me, which made me cry again. We sat lost and bewildered on the dirty old settee. None of us realised that soon Michael was to become Dad's main victim. He would be the star prize.

Michael and I saw Mum's bruises deepen before our eyes. Her neck bore overlapping fingerprints where Dad had struggled to get a firm grip as he'd tried to strangle her.

When Mum spoke, we saw a bottom tooth was missing, leaving a huge gap. Her arms were a mass of blue fingerprints and bruises. Clumps of hair stuck to her clothing. I looked at her head and saw bloodied bald patches where he'd tugged handfuls of her thick shiny hair out by the roots. "Oh Mum," I mouthed to her as I gripped her, not wanting to let her go, kissing her to make her better. She winced in pain at my gentle touch. "It'll be all right, we'll get through this," Mum told us nodding, trying to convince herself and us. I shook my head; it would get worse. False hope was not what we needed. Even we, as children knew that. "You're not to tell anyone," she said. "What happened stays within these walls; I have to sort this out, it's a family matter."

16 TRUMPET SOLO

Returning to my room, dazed and devastated, I climbed into bed and hugged my pillow for comfort. The severity of what happened hadn't sunk in. I understood nothing about any of it, all I could do was make comparisons with the kids at school, and their bullying behaviour which I was seeing a lot more of.

It would take a long time for me to recover from this if ever. What I knew was I would never forgive Dad, nor forget what he had done to us.

Michael was upset, his loud sobbing and shouting in his bedroom upset me further. He still had to rehearse for his debut concert in the city. People were travelling far and wide to see this concert, performed by young musicians. A lot depended on him, he was representing the school and the city, performing a trumpet solo. Michael wanted to call the Headmaster and cancel, so he could stay in the house to protect us. Mum wouldn't hear of it; "You can't let Mr. Evans and the school down, they're depending on you, the show must go on, your dad won't touch us again." I heard her making promises that even at my age, knew she couldn't keep. A minute later, Mum went to her room. I placed my ear on our adjoining bedroom wall, listening to her muffled sobs.

Mum's optimism hadn't convinced me. Dad's face had looked like he'd enjoyed every minute of it. The visions of dad's assaults on Mum tormented me. One minute I cried, the next I relived what I'd seen. None of it seemed real.

Michael rehearsed. His usual lively trumpet playing sounded more like a dirge. Tomorrow, he would play to a large audience of happy people, whilst his heart was breaking and his mind troubled. There was nothing I could do to help him, as I had a rehearsal too, mine was for something different.

Dragging my sore body out of my bed, I looked into my wardrobe mirror, trying hard to ignore my bloated, bruised face, and mimed… "My name is Hattie Thompson; Dad's hurt my mum and me. He tried to strangle my mum. He's destroyed the house. I am a witness and I tried to save my mum." It was painful to think about. I sobbed as I planned my speech. Someone had to help Mum, and as I'd seen it all, then it should be me. 'Be brave and fearless Hattie,' that's what Michael said, so I continued, determined to do this; "Our address is 32 Oak Road and my dad's name is Leonard Thompson and I don't want him to be my dad anymore." I'd written it all down. My usual practiced style looked ragged, but it was legible. I needed it written as I doubted my voice would return, nor would I be able to stop crying. I felt certain the Police officer would know something horrific had happened, by the state I was in, he'd know I wasn't lying.

My lack of a voice would prove I'd been screaming and my written statement would be evidence.

Michael came into my room. "What are you doing Hattie?" he asked, as I put my knitted cardigan on over my pyjamas, getting myself ready to leave the house. My eyes stung with fresh hot tears and my throat burned as I whispered in his ear; "I'm going to the police station. Dad needs locking up for trying to murder Mum and for vandalism." I knew what crimes he'd committed. I'd been watching police shows for months and I'd read newspapers Dad brought to the house on Sunday mornings. Michael had helped me with the difficult pronunciations, spellings, and together we looked up the meanings of the words, much to our horror, from reading the papers, we learned the world wasn't a very good place.

Mum stood by my door, eavesdropping, then came in; "What are you two chatterboxes up to?" she asked trying to make light of things even though she was in agony and could hardly stand. I cringed, at the sight of her injuries and her sad face, which set me off sobbing again. Michael told Mum what I was doing and said it made sense. He thought we should all go. Just because it was Dad, didn't mean he should get away with it, in fact, that was worse in our minds. "Hattie please don't go, I'll sort it out, I promise. You have been such a brave girl Hattie, but it's between Dad and me, it's an adult problem," Mum said.

Mum begged me until I gave in. It was all too much. I wasn't in a fit state to go anywhere. "One chance," I whispered, almost collapsing. I'd been through too much; my young mind seemed incapable of taking any more.

Taking one last glance in the mirror, I saw my cuteness had gone, wiped out in minutes because of Dad. My trusting eyes had become accusing and suspicious and my smiley mouth now tilted sadly down. I'd been through the wars and looked aged and haggard. Mum looked much worse. I'd never seen anyone look as damaged as Mum.

The overwhelming realisation of what we'd been through hit me again. Mum put me back into bed where I fitted for hours, she sat with me throughout. Every time I opened my eyes, I saw Mum, sobbing silently, staring at the window, her body shaking.

Later, when I woke, Mum said I had to stay off school until I was back to normal. Now I was being hidden because Dad was incapable of controlling his violent temper. My bruises were not to be seen, and I knew there was nothing *'normal'* about any of this. It made me wonder what Sally James would say if she'd seen me today. If I fought my Dad in such a way, to help Mum, then she had a big problem on her hands if she insisted on threatening and harassing me again. I'd cowered from her once, I would never cower again, not from anyone, regardless of size, age, or gender.

The next day Michael performed at the concert and returned exhausted, he'd done his best under the circumstances, no one noticed anything amiss. He'd hidden his worries well.

17 MUM GETS BUSY

Dad stayed away from the house for several days after his terrible first attack. We didn't know where he'd disappeared to; we were just glad he'd gone.

Mum tidied the house and packed a few things away as we were going on our first holiday during the long summer break which would soon be upon us, we were going to Italy. We had something to look forward to at last.

Mum repaired my torn yellow dress, she'd bought it for the trip, but Dad's violence had violated it, leaving me unsure if I could wear it. I packed it to please her; she said I should, in case I changed my mind. It was the prettiest dress I'd ever owned. Mum told us Dad's sister *'Aunt Jane'* was coming with us. She lived in America and would stay with us for most of the summer. My heart sank on hearing this news, I knew she'd be just like him, and her visit would be a terrible one.

18 FORCED TO PLAY

Dad returned to the house one Saturday morning to our horror. He went straight upstairs to his bedroom, banged and clattered for a while, then came downstairs, wearing a towel wrapped around his waist. He sat down on his worn armchair, blocking the television screen so no one else could see it. A minute later, he yelled; "Michael, get here now, it's trumpet time!" as he switched the television to another channel, and turned the volume up to its loudest setting. He seemed to be creating an atmosphere for something evil.

Michael ran downstairs, carrying his trumpet, he looked worried and frightened, when he came into the room, I'd never seen him look so scared. Watching him, I knew this hadn't been the first time Michael had been called to play like this. His actions looked as if he'd been playing under duress for some time. I'd seen kids react this way at school when they feared a teacher. Why hadn't he said anything?

Michael jumped to Dad's call, he knew the drill and began to play. I felt sick as I witnessed his, terrified, haunting performance, drowned out by the television. Michael's enthusiastic, bright happy face had changed. He looked mortified, nervous and his response seemed robotic.

Michael's free spirit was being stolen from him before my very eyes. How dare Dad do that, who the hell did he think he was to drain his son's soul? What had Dad done to him? What didn't I know?

I positioned myself close to my brother, so he knew he wasn't alone. My gut instincts were screaming out. Everything was wrong. We needed help.

When Michael played, Dad accompanied him, singing out of time and out of tune, attempting to sing in opera. The whole performance was bizarre, warped, and distressing to witness.

Dad sang made-up vile lyrics, of how he would beat us, and how he'd enjoyed doling out punches with the intent to kill us. He sang how later when our bodies were cold, he'd dance, sing, and spit on our graves, as he continued his perverse performance.

My brother played on in fear, as Dad attempted to hold on to his extra-large towel in a peculiar display, trying to mimic a matador. I could only watch on aghast at his obscenities.

Dad pathetically attempted to grasp the towel ends as it dropped from his waist to the floor during a succession of twirls. We saw Dad in a way that terrified us. He re-wrapped his towel over his naked person, unabashed, then said; "Now play this one," as he hummed a tune which Michael had to replicate even though it wasn't a familiar tune. This was a sick game, in which Dad was trying to humiliate Michael and destroy his confidence. Dad's ambition to scare us had worked; it petrified us.

"No Dad, I don't want to play anymore, I've played eight times. My lips are sore," Michael told him.

"I said play the sodding tune, you'll do as you're bloody well told," Dad hissed. "You're in my bloody house, so you'll do what I say when I say it, or I'll give you what for. Now play it," and off he pranced again, shamelessly. Dad's face looked demonic, a smirk quivered on his thin mean lips, he looked triumphant as he got his own way. His abusive hands conducted an invisible orchestra as Michael fought back tears and I watched seething, heartbroken, and disgusted.

This became one of dad's Saturday morning rituals.

19 REVENGE

It seemed Dad was getting away with the many violent physical and mental abuses he inflicted on us which continued for many years. Mum seemed too forgiving, making excuses for Dad's behavior, which we could not accept nor understand, yet there was a sinister reason for Mum's silence which we wouldn't find out until many years later. Only then would we understand her silence, her brave sacrifices, and what she'd endured, to keep us alive.

As no one appeared to be seeking justice for Dad's criminal abuses, I punished him myself. My plan was not original; Shirley Mason told me she used this punishment on her brother when he stole her pocket money.

I spat in his food and cups of tea from that day on, knowing I'd get a big smack if I got caught, but I did it anyway, at every opportunity. It seemed well worth the risk. I wanted to make him stop, but I didn't know how to.

A few days after the attack, we sat around the old dining table as Dad insisted, we do. I struggled to sit 'properly,' feeling a fit of laughter brewing because I'd spat in his food and mixed in a dead spider, this amused me no end, as I watched Dad tuck into his food greedily.

Dad chomped noisily, slopping his food all over himself and the table. He'd stare at the food on his plate, then stab at it with his fork, munching with his sloppy mouth wide open as my brother and I stared at the food rotating in his open mouth. Michael and I found it fascinating in a repulsive kind of way. The kids at school ate better than he did, and they were disgusting. Some ate that way to shock everyone, others knew no different.

I wondered what Dad would do if he knew what he'd gobbled down.

Dad was vulgar around us, but Michael and I knew he was a well-mannered gentleman, away from the house, as we accompanied him to what I believed was a posh restaurant a short time ago. He said it was; a work's do.

Dad was very polite in the restaurant, he used good manners both at the table and with the other guests. We were impressed at how popular and funny Dad was and how people fawned all over him. Everyone seemed to like him.

Strangers came to our table to talk to Dad. Most were attractive, loud young ladies. I thought they might be models or actresses. All had fake, thick eyelashes on that were so long they almost reached their eyebrows. To me, they looked like pandas and caterpillars.

Dad seemed to like everybody here in this restaurant. He took his camera out of its case, put a new flash on top, then wandered around the dim-lit room, taking his camera with him, leaving Michael and me alone. We felt abandoned as Dad blended in with the guests.

There were no other kids in there, which we thought was strange as it was supposed to be a family occasion like the other times. All I saw were adults sitting at candlelit tables looking cosy, some were kissing and touching each other which I thought was odd. Others were dancing in the middle of the room, to slow music, they hardly moved.

Dad walked around the room as Michael and I gazed on, our eyes never left him, as we watched every move he made, wishing he would come back to us.

I saw beautiful women and handsome men jump out of their chairs and pose; they looked funny as they made strange faces for the camera. Some of them rubbed his arm. "Oh Lenny, please take my photograph, please, pretty please," One lady gushed. I wondered why she sounded like a child when she looked as old as Mum.

Everyone shouted and laughed loudly as the music played softly in the background. I understood none of it, nor did I like it there, it didn't feel right. My instincts told me I was in a bad place for reasons I didn't understand. "Is this a restaurant?" I asked Michael who looked at me with a worried expression. He seemed to dither... "No, it's a brothel," he whispered. That information meant nothing to me. I had no idea what a brothel was. Michael didn't know how to explain it to me. I understood it was a terrible place and Dad was bad for taking us there and bad for lying. He'd told Mum we were going to a restaurant.

My decision to punish Dad for hurting us and going to that brothel seemed justified. One spit for each crime would be a good start for his disgraceful behaviour. I watched him shovel fork loads of food into his chomping mouth. He glugged down his tea laced with phlegm. I observed with devilment and self-pride.

As Dad continued scoffing, he broke wind, with satisfaction, then took out his handkerchief from his trouser pocket, and wiped his mouth. All the time I watched in disgust as he used that dirty rag, caked in hard green snot, that he'd used several times a day and pocketed for weeks, his belly was full. Dad was content, and we were disgusted.

That'll teach him. A vile punishment for a disgusting man I gloated to myself. I felt my mischievous sparkle return, then I knew whatever he did, I wouldn't lose my spirit. I hoped mum and Michael would keep theirs too.

Mum would be furious if she knew what I'd done. I tried to tell Michael my secret by flicking my eyes sideways towards Dad, encouraging him to look, but there was nothing to see. I was becoming hysterical as giggles brewed in the pit of my stomach. Michael kicked me under the table to warn me to be quiet, he knew I'd done something silly.

After we cleared the messy table, Michael came into my bedroom. "What the heck have you done Hattie?" he asked, concerned.

I spat in Dad's food and drinks, to punish him for hurting you and Mum, and for taking us to the brothel."

"You, shouldn't do that Hattie, he won't know, so it won't make any difference, and If he finds out, he'll batter you. You know what he's like, don't provoke him," advised Michael.

"It's already made a massive difference," I stated, smug and triumphant, my voice croaking, it was still early days after the violent attack and I needed revenge, anyway I could get it. "He's a disgrace and no one's telling the police. Why should he get away with hurting us? He told us bad people should get punished, and he's terrible and isn't getting into any trouble, from anyone. I'll punish him every day," I stated.

Mum had been listening. She stormed into my room, took hold of me, and looked into my eyes; "You'll stop that disgusting nonsense right now Hattie Thompson!" Then I got my legs smacked, hard enough to humiliate me and make me cry. I was furious. "So, you can punish me and not him for bullying you and upsetting me. I've just given him a little punishment for huge crimes. He should be in prison." I shouted, gulping down the sobs, flabbergasted I hadn't received the praise I deserved. "You should thank me, not smack my legs," I yelled.

"It's disgusting behavior, Hattie you can't go around spitting in food and drink, two wrongs don't make a right," shouted Mum.

"He's bloody disgusting, a pig and a bully," I yelled back. "Tell the police he's bad. You're terrible for not telling, you're wrong. He'll kill us. Why don't you do something?"

"Hattie, get to bed, right now, and stay there until I say you can come down. If you swear one more time, there'll be trouble," Mum yelled, with her hands on her hips.

"It's bad enough having one vile person in the house, we don't need two."

"We don't need him and we don't want him. Why did you marry him? Report him," I shouted at her, getting the last word in, then flopped onto my old bed, belly down, kicking my legs up and down in a rage of frustration and fear.

20 DENTISTS

With the forthcoming visit of Aunt Jane, life in the house needed to appear normal for the duration of her stay. We would have to live a lie. Our problems needed to remain a secret and put on hold, and any evidence of Dad's outbursts needed to be hidden.

To disguise obvious evidence of Dad's violence against Mum, she bought bottles of Witch Hazel to help take the colour out of her bruises, and she bought a thick, cheap foundation to cover her face and neck, none of which helped.

Mum went to the local dental surgery to have a crown put in to replace the missing tooth Dad punched out. I went with her, witnessing her embarrassment. She hadn't wanted to go but Dad insisted; he didn't want his sister asking questions as the answers would upset her stay. "There's a bloody big gap," he'd yelled as if the gap was Mum's fault. "Get the sodding thing sorted out before Janie gets here!" he raged, without giving her the money to pay for the damage he'd inflicted.

In the Dentist's surgery, I watched Mum from the corner of the room, as Dr. Oldham examined her mouth... "Mrs. Thompson, what on earth has happened to you?" He asked, with concern, as he peered into her mouth with a tiny torch strapped on his head. That was the perfect cue, if she told him what happened, we'd be able to get help, he'd write it down as evidence for the police.

Mum lied. She gave him the classic excuse; She'd fallen down the stairs, using a stock answer, the same as all the other battered toothless wives gave, just as Michael had predicted.

I'd asked Michael earlier what he thought Mum would say if the dentist asked what happened. "I think she'll say she fell down the stairs or bumped into a door, they all say it thinking no one will suspect, but the dentist will know, it's obvious."

My hope had been for her to be honest and say; "My husband punched it out when he was attacking me," but she didn't dare.

The Dentist's face showed disbelief as mum uttered her excuse. I gasped aloud and glared at her, furious she hadn't taken the cue and angry she'd lied on Dad's behalf.

It was hard for me to keep quiet and not blurt out the truth. Mum glowered at me, ordering me to remain silent.

The dentist examined her bruises and abrasions. Her bottom lip still swollen, Dr. Oldham must have seen hundreds of fat lips, even I had. All the kids at school had, by the school gates where parents waited to collect their children. The parents would laugh and pretend life was great, but their injuries confirmed it wasn't great at all.

Michael and I had seen it all, black eyes, hair missing, fat lips, cuts, bruises, ripped clothes. It wasn't only women who got beaten, the men also bore the occasional black eye. Some parents looked fine at nine in the morning and a bloody mess by four in the afternoon.

Even as kids, we knew what was happening, and we knew these bruised parents weren't falling down or bumping into doors and few sought any help, they put up with it as they were too scared to say anything. No one spoke out, so nothing got done.

It seemed most people worried more about what the neighbours might say. Others were scared the police would come around to take their spouse away in the back of a police van. I knew because I'd heard them down our road. One day I saw the police had hold of Bert Johnson, about to put the cuffs on him. He'd beaten his wife to a pulp, and she was on the road in front of the police car, blood all over her face, as she screamed; "Don't take him, I love him." The police let him go and Nora Johnson got fined for wasting police time. Bert was let off with a verbal warning, that's what I heard a neighbour tell Mum. He battered her again the next day. Sometimes it was the other way around, like with Jan Sharp. She beat her husband up really badly. The tongues never stopped wagging after that.

Once the dentist had finished attending to Mum, he told the receptionist to calculate the cost of the dental work, which entailed tidying up a brutalised mouth, gums, and analysing the dimensions of the crown which would be ready in a few days.

Mum emptied her purse of coins onto the counter to make her first payment. Several pennies rolled in different directions on the floor, heightening our embarrassment. We dropped onto our hands and knees to retrieve the rolling coins. Mum's face had turned bright red with shame she shouldn't have had.

Mum looked shocked when she heard the price of the crown. It would be costly and Mum would have to pay for it in installments over several months.

After the summer break, Mum was to start work, it seemed her wages would be needed to pay for the crown, and ongoing treatment for the injuries Dad had inflicted. I felt gutted for her; I couldn't imagine how she felt.

21 COUNTING DOWN THE DAYS

Michael and I were counting down the days until Aunt Jane's arrival. Part of us looked forward to her visit, the other part dreaded it. Both of us had high expectations of her; from watching American television shows such as *Here's Lucy*, and *The Big Valley*. Neither of us knew anything about her, only that she was to stay with us for the summer and come to Italy with us.

Dad's forewarning to Michael and me was to keep out of the way and be quiet at all times. I wondered why she would want that, wasn't she coming to get to know us? didn't she like kids? No doubt we would soon find out.

I walked into the living room to find Mum sitting on the floor with Michael. Mum was trying to plan the route for the trip as she would be the navigator. She was leaning over a huge world map which was so creased; I didn't know how she would ever fold it again. "England is here, and Italy is there," she said enthusiastically, bouncing her finger between both countries. "Italy is shaped like a boot, and we are going to its heel for three weeks, to a lovely city called Taranto. Your Dad wants to visit a friend called Clelia."

We could hardly contain our excitement, we had something to look forward to, an adventure.

22 CHOCOLATES

Mum kept me off school for three weeks, as my bruises were obvious and would no doubt have drawn huge attention to our secret plight. I'd needed time to heal. My voice was returning to normal, apart from a slight stutter I didn't normally have. I was sufficiently calm during the day though nights were tumultuous. The shocking events at the house were hard for me to deal with.

We were victims now, with scars and bruises. Our lives had changed. I'd been a happy girl just weeks ago, now because of Dad, I'd become a terrified, hurt, and miserable one.

Mum said I could return to school on the last day of the school year. I'd no idea how to explain my absence, stutter, and sad eyes if anyone asked. There would be a fancy-dress party on this day. Michael and I didn't want to dress up nor did we want to go. We needed to stay on guard at the house.

Mum warned me to keep quiet, regarding what happened at the hands of Dad. "Why can't I tell the teachers what happened, when they ask why I haven't been at school, you know I don't lie?" I demanded to know.

"Because your dad will get into serious trouble, and it's not anyone's business," said Mum, concerned I'd blab and cause chaos, like Donna Perkins, had done. Donna had spoken out regarding her violent father, soon after, she and her siblings were taken to live with foster parents. We never saw or heard from them ever again.

To prepare for the party, Mum had daubed thick tacky makeup all over my face. She tried to cover evidence of bruising, just as she had when we went to the dentists. As I watched her, I felt shocked to see how many bruises she still had. I doubted she would ever heal. Her face was still bloated. It grieved me to look at her. She'd only left the house once, to see the dentist.

"I'll look ridiculous!" I exclaimed as none of the makeup had been blended in. "It's orange and you can see lines," I moaned as I looked into the tiny shaving mirror in the bathroom.

"No, you won't, you'll look lovely Hattie," Mum tried to assure me, but she was fibbing, I looked horrendous and felt even worse.

Michael and I sneaked into the school hall late. The party was well underway. We hoped we wouldn't be seen, but Mrs. Dixon the deputy head spotted us. She beckoned us to follow her to her office, just before a fresh game of musical chairs began.

At first, we thought we'd done something wrong, and stood by her desk feeling nervous. To our surprise, she handed us a small box of chocolates each, the fancy handmade ones we'd seen advertised on television, but would never have been able to afford.

"Your father took some splendid photographs for me and didn't want me to pay, so I've bought you, these," she said handing us a fancy decorated box each.

"Whatever you do, don't let the other children see them. They may think its favouritism," she whispered as she looked at me with a strange expression. I was sure she'd seen the bruising under the patchy foundation. She stared at my right cheek and frowned. "You know something, you two are such lucky children, you have a wonderful kind Dad. It's so sad that many children in this school aren't as fortunate," she added, as her eyes teared up.

"The photographs he took for me are fantastic, and he's ever so funny... yes, a delightful man, an absolute hoot," she gushed, looking amused and besotted, remembering something hilarious he must have said. "I can't thank him enough. Give him my regards children, when you get home, and Hattie, no more scrapes, your father has enough to do, without worrying about you," she said, wagging a finger at me. My legs almost gave way, I hadn't been in any scrapes. I'd been thrown across the room, trying to save Mum from my evil father, who Mrs. Dixon thought was delightful.

I was dying to blurt out everything, then remembered, I had to keep quiet. It was doubtful she'd believe me. According to other kids, she believed no one other than teachers and grownups. Just by looking at her gullible smitten face, it was obvious she'd fallen for his act and convincing lies. If only Mum hadn't put foundation on me to cover the bruises on my face, she'd see the handprints were adult size, those of a large man; Dad!

"She adores him," I said to Michael, once out of her office. He was as shocked as I was.

"If only she knew the truth," said Michael. It was obvious Dad was a good liar and a great actor. He'd twisted things to his own advantage and Mrs. Dixon was naïve to not see through him. How many others were there just like her? I remembered her turning a blind eye on those horrid teachers who pushed our sleeves up to thrash us on our forearms. She'd walked into the classroom and straight back out again, pretending she hadn't seen anything.

Now we knew how Dad got people to like him, we'd watched his tactics at the brothel's restaurant. His trick was to take free photographs, and Mrs. Dixon had validated that fact.

Dad was well known, a trusted photographer, funny, charming, and manipulative. I'd tagged along to his freelance jobs, watching how he got people doing what he wanted them to do, at weddings and other special events, it was quite an education for a child.

"He's set us all up, covered his back, she'll be against us, Mrs. Dixon's on his side and will never listen to a wrong word said about him, she'll think we're to blame for the bruises," said Michael.

"I bet he's lied to our Uncles and Aunties and all of Mum's friends, that's why they never bother with us anymore.

After discussing Dad's deviousness and the gullibility of our deputy head, who'd been played, and bought with free photographs, we hid our chocolates in our school bags.

Sally James had been watching every move we made, unaware I'd noticed her hiding behind the coats in the open cloakroom. I'd spotted her snooping earlier and felt tempted to pull the coats off their hangers and shout *BOO!* but decided not to bother.

We returned to the party where we played as never before.

The school bell rang to end the celebrations and the school year. We and the other children charged out through the tall school gates screaming with joy as everyone headed to their respective houses.

Michael and I stood stock still at the gate, reluctant to go back to the house, so we headed to the local hardware shop and bought a fishing net with our emergency money. We went to catch newts at the nearby pond. Once there, we ate our chocolates in silence and slipped slimy newts into an empty jam jar, then put them back into the water when we'd had enough fishing.

On our return to the house after hours of fun, we found Mum crying in her room. beneath her bed covers. She refused to look at us, or speak. We slipped out of the room in silence, both of us shaken, not knowing what to do.

Dad was out somewhere. A chair was upside down in the living room. The clock was in pieces on the hearth. The eeriness of fear in the air was overpowering. How we wished we hadn't gone to the party or the pond. I wondered what Mrs. Dixon would have to say if she'd seen what the hilarious photographer had done to his wife. She'd know for certain he wasn't a *hoot* at all, and we were unfortunate, not the lucky ones she'd assumed us to be.

23 LAST ATTACKS FOR NOW

Dad waited until the school break before he set about physically bullying Mum and Michael more frequently, getting his last-minute attacks in before his sister arrived. There was no one around to question the injuries. Now school had finished for the summer it gave Dad a free rein to do what he liked most; beating his wife and son in various degrees. Each act of cruelty merged into the next. He aimed his punches to their lower bodies, to hide the evidence. Sometimes I bore witness, other times I would return to see the horrific aftermath of yet another brutal assault. This was our way of life now.

Dad attacked me too, though not to the same degree as Mum and Michael, but still terrible. He shouted at me one time; "I've bloody warned you, Hattie Thompson, I'm bloody well sick of you. You never shut up, you're a bloody busybody, a little know it all." Then he kicked me hard on the backside, yanked me up into the air and shook me for what seemed like an eternity, then threw me into the fireplace, as I screamed hysterically, got up, and tried to kick him as he laughed and taunted me. Dad seemed proud and amused as he watched my efforts to fight back. It seemed I entertained him. Whereas Mum and Michael were a challenge to him, that needed conquering.

24 A STERN WARNING

Dad was beside himself with excitement over his sister's forthcoming visit and before she arrived; gave us another stern warning... "If you do one bloody thing I don't like when my sister Janey is here, I swear, I'll kill the bloody lot of you. You two, stay in Michael's bedroom and come down only when I tell you to. No cheek and speak only when you're spoken to, or I swear it'll be the last thing you ever do. Do you get that?" We nodded. He described what he would do to us in the vilest, most explicit ways, depicting how he would murder us, smiling, as he lost himself in the details. Our terrified, disgusted young faces stared at him in horror. We couldn't understand his chain of thought, as we were good kids and he was trying to persuade us otherwise, which made no sense. Michael and I weren't falling for his brainwashing, not like the deputy headmistress had, and the rest of his followers.

Who was Dad to tell us how to behave? Didn't he realise he was not setting a good example? We were strong-minded children, for our ages, we could see right through him, and we were having none of it!

25 WHAT'S WRONG DADDY?

Being the sort of child that leaps in where angels feared to tread, I came up with an idea to sort things out, or at least try, I told Michael; "I'll ask Dad what's wrong with him." I was so fed up and worried, with all the shouting, screaming, and violence, it was making me ill.

"No Hattie, he's mad, he'll hurt you," cautioned Michael.

"Not if I put my tiara and my princess slippers on," I told him as I ran off to put them on. I hadn't worn them since my sixth birthday. I had hoped for a surprise party, one where everyone jumped out with balloons and a cake with six lit candles. Sadly, there hadn't been a party or a cake.

I thought if I dressed up as a princess, then Dad might remember the days when he loved us. If I made him tell me what was wrong, then we could fix it. Michael tried to stop me from approaching Dad. He knew I was taking a huge risk and said it was a dangerous idea, but nothing would stop me, I needed to talk to Dad. If anyone could get around him and find out his problem, I guessed it would be me, he didn't hate me as much as Michael and Mum.

Whilst I still had the courage, I put my tiara on, found my princess slippers, which I had outgrown and I clip-clopped downstairs with Michael.

"Michael, you hide, get the biggest pan you can find. If he hurts me, I'll shout, as loud as I can. Then come in and hit him on the head with it," I instructed him.

Michael agreed as I clomped into the living room, wearing a fake smile. Dad was sat in his chair, his snotty cotton handkerchief stuffed down its side with his newspaper; I stood for a moment and took a deep breath before I made my move. He was half watching television and nodding off, giving an occasional grunt. Michael was in the hallway, prepared, and ready for the worse. I climbed onto Dad's knee as if nothing bad had ever happened. It was terrifying and my actions made me feel sick, but I sat on his knee and smiled up at him. He smiled back and snuggled further into his chair, helping me get cosy.

"Well Hi there Princess Hattie, how are you today?" he asked, looking pleased to see me.

"I'm fine Daddy, thank you," I answered, politely, snuggling against him, pretending to watch television. Once I decided he seemed happy enough for me to talk to him, I began; "I need to ask you something, Daddy."

"OK, Hattie, what would you like to know? Fire away."

"Well it's very serious Daddy and I don't want you to shout."

"Okay, I promise I won't shout," he said, amused.

"Do you Daddy?"

"Yes, I promise, cross my heart and hope to die," he was enjoying this game. How I wished I didn't need to make him play it. I missed the Dad I had not so long ago, but I had to think of now. Everything had changed for the worse. I didn't know if I was doing the right thing or not, but I needed to know what he had to say for himself. I had to stop him. The only way I could think of was to face him and say it... "Well Daddy, I want to know if you will stop shouting and hurting us. We don't like it. We are afraid of you." I looked him in the eye as I told him. "You used to be so nice and so much fun, we don't know why you changed, or why you are hurting us. Please, Daddy, tell me why you're doing these terrible things. Why do you hate us so much? what happened?"

For a fleeting moment Dad looked guilty, he coughed as if embarrassed, then rose out of his chair giving me a little push off his knee, and left the room. Moments later, the front door slammed, he'd run off, without answering my questions.

"You're brave Hattie, I'm proud of you," Michael said, relieved I had returned to him in one piece. Dad didn't return until the next day, perhaps I'd shamed him, perhaps not, at least I'd tried. Sadly, my effort made no difference.

26 CALL FOR HELP

Mum continued promising things would get better with Dad. She believed him when he said sorry. Michael and I witnessed him grovel for forgiveness, we found him pathetic. Dad was a compulsive liar who was tormenting Mum in the cruellest ways possible. He'd lied in the same way as the kids at school did, avoiding eye contact, using a high-pitched voice, and putting on the tears.

One afternoon, Mum helped me tidy my wardrobes, to make room for several dresses she'd bought for me from a local jumble sale. The dresses were new to me, but old and unwanted by the person who'd donated them. "Most of these dresses will be perfect for school when you start back after the summer. The bright flowery ones will be lovely for the holiday," she said, trying to raise a smile out of me, but all I could think about were the problems we needed to sort out, not dresses.

Mum was suffering yet she tried to stay positive. My lips trembled as I watched her, touched by her enthusiasm and love for me. I cried. Mum's expression changed to one of immense sadness. To my surprise she whispered; "We must get help; this can't go on. I look at your faces, you are both so frightened, so sad. I'm going to call Uncle Barry, while Dad is out, this has to stop. Don't tell your dad." She didn't need to warn me; I had no intention of speaking to Dad ever again.

At last, I felt a glimmer of hope; Mum would get us the help we needed, then we could get back to leading a normal life.

27 UNCLE BARRY'S COMING

Michael had been asking mum for weeks; "Is there anyone who can help us?" Mum didn't think so. Family and friends had all stopped making contact. It was as if no one wanted us anymore.

We hoped Uncle Barry would help us, he seemed the strongest and most dependable one in the family, according to Mum. She'd told us many stories of how Uncle Barry had looked after her, and their younger siblings whilst growing up when Pop and Gran were working, and how reliable he was. He was our only hope, there was no one else.

Uncle Barry was married to Aunt Laura, they had two sons, Ryan and Richard. They'd always been my favourite cousins, they used to visit us on special occasions. Sometimes they brought us a gift each. The younger cousin, Richard was my favourite. He used to torment and tease me. Ryan was the comedian, we would roar with laughter at his jokes, but he never wanted to come out on the bikes or roller skate, he preferred to read his comics. I hoped Uncle Barry would bring them if he came.

Dad was away taking photographs. He'd taken a lot of equipment with him, special lenses, tripods, three cameras, and a few boxes of film. This time he took the car, so we knew he had a time-consuming assignment. This seemed the perfect time for Mum to make her desperate phone call to Uncle Barry. Michael and I stood by her side in silence, so she could concentrate on what she had to say. She was on the verge of tears as she tapped out his telephone number as the lock was on the phone's dial, another of Dad's attempts to prevent us from connecting to the outside world, that place was only for him. He had no idea we tapped out the numbers rather than dialling, which made his lock worthless. Michael had shown us how, having figured it out in a matter of minutes.

"*It's ringing,*" Mum whispered, as we put our heads close to the earpiece to listen, looking at each other with eyes filled with hope." Barry, it's me, Helen, your sister. I'm sorry to bother you, but we need help." Mum said as tears poured down her face. Her voice broke as she struggled to calm herself. She was desperate. "*Please help us,*" Mum pleaded. Our hearts were pounding, fifty to the dozen as we stood, hopeful, by her side. We felt bad for her, as she sought protection and support, for us. "Len's hurting the children and me, it's been going on for almost two months now, I don't know what to do." We put our arms around her waist to give her our support. I could feel her shaking. Mum's sobs were distressing. We cried too, feeling small, helpless, and hopeless as we watched her. All three of us were full of hope that Uncle Barry would help us.

Dad had reduced Mum to a sad desperate lady, on the verge of being destroyed.

"Calm down Helen. Please, shush now. It's doubtful I can get over, so I can't make any promises," said Uncle Barry in his loud baritone voice. "I'm a very busy man. My family needs me with them as I work overseas a lot; the boys want me at weekends, that's the only time I can be with them. They go horse riding and do so many other sports, and to be honest, I like to be there for them." His deep voice spoke over Mum's, dominating the entire conversation, making it about him, his family, and their activities. He was on a roll, boasting how well they were all doing.

We learned that Aunt Laura was busy with all her voluntary work, baking cakes, and scones for the local animal rescue society. The boys would go on school exchange trips soon. Ryan was off to Switzerland. "Ryan will ski every day," gushed Uncle Barry. "He's able to ski down the black runs now. Hmm.... he's very advanced, an accomplished young man."

Uncle Barry appeared to be talking to himself, he seemed to have forgotten Mum was at the end of the line. Richard was flying off to France to sightsee and practice his language skills. "Oh yes, he's an amazing lad, fluent in French. It will be a marvellous experience for him to practice the language over there and not just read from a textbook." He bragged nonstop for almost an hour, he wouldn't stop talking over Mum, as she tried to tell him what Dad was doing to us all.

Mum had to stop Uncle Barry from continuing, as she was running up a huge telephone bill. Dad would go ballistic when the next itemized phone bill dropped through the letter-box, then our secret calls would be discovered, and we'd get another beating. It didn't bear thinking about. It was obvious Uncle Barry would not come; he was too busy. Mum was wasting her time asking.

Mum apologised; "Barry, you're busy, I'm so sorry I asked, but I had no one else to turn to, please, just forget I called. Don't worry, you have your family. I had no right to intrude. Perhaps Len will back off now his sister is coming to stay. I'll let you go now. I'm so sorry, give my love to the family." That statement changed the conversation; he'd stopped spouting and listened, then said; "I think I might manage a short trip. ... When did you say Jane is arriving?" Mum told him Aunt Jane would arrive in two days.

"Hmm. ... I reckon I can get there on Friday evening, stay a few days, I'll see what I can do. I'll book in at a hotel nearby, yes, that's what I'll do." The call ended as tears of gratitude and relief poured down Mum's cheeks. We cuddled her hard as she fought back her sobs.

At last, we had support, someone who cared about our plight, our uncle was coming to help us.

Mum thanked him over and over, for agreeing to take time out of his busy life to help us sort out our miserable one. They said their goodbyes and hung up.

"Don't expect too much Hattie, he's coming to see Aunt Jane. He doesn't give a damn about us," said Michael wisely.

28 AUNT JANE'S ARRIVAL

The day we had been waiting for was upon us. We'd only just finished trying to make a disgusting living room look halfway decent, to prepare for Aunt Jane's arrival, when the sound of a taxi honking its horn outside, let us know Aunt Jane from America had arrived. Michael and I ran outside, as did several of the neighbours, to see what was going on.

We saw a fancy lady standing by the taxi. She had a red set of five suitcases piled high in various sizes. She looked nervous and impatient as she made her way to the gate, then stood poised, waiting for the taxi driver to open it for her. Once he'd opened the gate for her, she waltzed down our path as if on a catwalk, and headed towards our ghastly shocking pink coloured front door, followed by the cabby who struggled to carry the set of luggage. She offered him no help.

One boy, Eddie from next door, seemed to become overexcited as he stood on the porch attached to ours. He yelled out for all to hear; "Look at her, its lady bloody muck arriving, she reckons the cabbies her very own bloody butler." A couple of his family members roared with cackling laughter. "She won't help him with her own cases, the rotten cow." He shouted in a voice on the verge of breaking. Eddie looked around, seeking approval for his outburst, then flicked his rolled-up cigarette stump into our lupines as several other family members piled out of the house. They formed a large group of jeering onlookers, all whistling, catcalling, and laughing at Aunt Jane's Hollywood-style arrival. It was hard to tell if they were admiring her, jealous of her, or mocking her. Aunt Jane spun around on her heels. "Do I know any of you?" She asked, in a gritty deep voice with an amazing drawl which I liked a lot. "No, I don't," she answered for them. "Then I suggest you all shut the fuck up!" We weren't expecting her to give such a response. We and the neighbours realised she was feisty and not as weak and demure as she looked.

"Bloody hell, get a load of her," called another neighbour.

The boy and his family came further out of their huddled group and spread out, some along their path. Others stayed in the middle of their garden where they had an old motorbike and a mouldy old, urine-stained mattress which another brother jumped up and down on, shouting; "Come on over 'ere and lay down we' me, lady," whilst another boy sat on the motorbike, goading Aunt Jane further, as she made her debut arrival. I hid behind Michael, giggling, some of their comments were hilarious.

"Av you saw 'err, are kid?" one of them asked another.

"She thinks she's posh." Shouted another as they continued making rude comments and vulgar sounds.

I realised they were threatening, as my giggles stopped and I became scared.

"I'd giver one, give that one a bloody good ride around the block, bet she's ad a few. She looks like she's bin around the block a few times already," shouted Stevie, now sitting on the old motorbike, as his family howled with laughter.

The oldest brother was away on holiday, that's what their mother said, in fact, a few of the mothers down our road said the same about members of their families, I used to think them lucky to have such long holidays until Maureen Green told me they were in prison and not on holiday.

The three sisters from next door kept quiet as they watched our Aunt in awe. One held a tiny baby.

"You're disgusting, a horrible rude thug!" snarled Aunt Jane, who found herself drowned out by more catcalls and laughter.

"I'll show ya what rude is anytime ya want lady," one of them sneered, making obscene gestures towards her, laughing. Aunt Jane flew into the house through our door, visibly shaken, her face flushed with rage and embarrassment, this was not the welcome she'd expected.

The taxi driver was still on our path waiting for his fare, he seemed to have been forgotten, until Mum noticed him, and asked if he was all right, he smiled at her concern, as she rummaged through her purse to pay him, worried she wouldn't have money for the fare and shaken by the neighbours' dreadful behaviour. I felt sad as I watched her scrape through her purse, knowing that would be the last money she'd have in there for a week; until the child benefit came through.

Mum pushed her fingers into the creases of her tatty plastic purse trying to get her loose coins to the correct amount, unable to tip the taxi driver. It was obvious Aunt Jane would not pay for her own journey. The taxi driver looked at Mum, almost in sympathy. He didn't seem to mind that there wasn't enough for a tip; he looked relieved to be on his way. "Good luck with that one Luv," he said, gesturing towards Aunt Jane with his head. Mum smiled politely, as she returned into the house, shutting the door on the din from the baying mob who lived next door.

29 THE FAMILY NEXT DOOR

The family next door remained at the top of our path, swearing, shouting, and larking about for hours, it seemed they were there for the unforeseeable future. Now, Aunt Jane was here, they would watch her nonstop until the end of her stay.

Since the Smiths moved in, we'd heard strange noises in the middle of the night, dragging sounds outside. I thought they were shifting dead bodies or swag from the large vans which pulled up around three in the morning. The noises often woke me. I peeped through my window once and saw them dragging bundles towards their alley. I was so scared they'd see me. We'd heard other strange sounds too, which appeared to come from the loft, a constant banging and shuffling. I would lie on my tiny bed staring at the ceiling, worried someone would drop onto my bed. There was so much to fear in our house, with Dad, and the neighbours. Mum said she was surprised the police weren't next-door every night. "Why are you surprised, Mum?" I asked.

"Because they're always fighting and shouting, it sounds like they're killing each other."

"Like Dad!" I blurted, hoping she'd recognise the comparison and call the Police.

30 A FORMAL INTRODUCTION

Aunt Jane followed Mum and me upstairs to see my box room where she would sleep during her stay. I would share Michael's room and sleep on a little old camp bed.

We left Aunt Jane to unpack and freshen up, it had been a long journey from New York to England, she might be tired and want a nap, so left her to her own devices.

Half an hour later, we heard Aunt Jane hollering; "Michael, Hattie, get here right now!" She sounded bossy and impatient. It seemed the tone she used was to inform us she was another boss in charge of us. We ran inside the house, to find her in the living room. Michael and I stood side by side, almost to attention, waiting for her to speak. "Well children, as if you don't already know, I'm Aunt Jane," she announced, using a more pleasant tone; "Do you want to ask me anything?" As she spoke, the stench of tobacco, hit us full-on, her breath and clothes stank. I would have liked to ask Aunt Jane why she was here and if she was going to be nasty like Dad? but I kept quiet, waiting to be dismissed.

Aunt Jane seemed nervous, puffing on her cigarettes nonstop. She stubbed one out, then immediately lit another.

I wanted to leave the polluted room to avoid the smoke, which she deliberately blew into our faces as she stared at us, coldly, weighing us up. We'd never met anyone like her. I stared at her, observing everything about her. Michael noticed what I was doing and dropped a bombshell. He whispered in my ear; "She's wearing a wig, and she's got gold teeth." I lost control immediately and burst out laughing, unable to stop myself, I hadn't got that far with my scrutinising yet. Aunt Jane glared at me and made me laugh even more. She was losing patience, with me. Her poised, sophisticated act slipped before our eyes. It was obvious I vexed her, as her nostrils flared at a speed I'd never seen before, with smoke puffing out, sending Michael and me deeper into hysterics.

Michael whispered, "She's a dragon," and that finished me off, I was almost rolling on the floor with hearty belly laughs, as was Michael. We couldn't stop, it wasn't nerves making us laugh, it was her. She became furious and fled upstairs before imploding. Michael looked at me, amused. On cue, we flared our nostrils; our full hearty laughs erupted like a volcano. It was obvious she was one of those people without a sense of humour who I felt so sad for. At least we'd be able to tell when she was getting angry, the flaring nostrils were the giveaway.

Later, when Aunt Jane came down, I took another good look at her. She looked like a model from a fashion magazine. I was in awe of the way she walked and dressed. She looked business-like, stylish, and successful. Her clothes were beautiful; it wasn't surprising she had attracted attention from the neighbours. None of us had ever seen anyone like her before, certainly not down our road.

My first impression of her had not been a good one, and I wouldn't be giving her a second chance to make another, I couldn't take that risk. My gut instincts told me, she was evil, like Dad.

31 DAD APPEARS

Dad came bounding in, out of nowhere. "Oh Janie, darling, how fabulous to have yar here at long last, you look wonderful, it's bin so long." He sounded like cousin Katie, putting on the same new accent, with a mix of the old one, sounding hilarious, which set Michael and me off laughing again. I didn't know how we would cope with all this drama and phoniness.

Aunt Jane hadn't said one word to Mum, who was sitting on the settee, so Michael and I snuggled up next to her and told her we loved her. "Be careful you two. Try to keep your giggles under control, especially you Hattie. Say nothing that will give them cause to lose their tempers. They don't have the same sense of humour as us and don't forget Aunt Jane isn't used to children. Be on your guard. Look after one another. I love you both. Let's get through this visit, as best as we can," said Mum. Her warning didn't sound good, alarm bells rang in my head. This would not be pleasurable; it would be an ordeal.

32 NEW CLOTHES & NASTY NIPS

The next day, Dad and Aunt Jane disappeared from the house for hours. On their return, Dad was sporting a new suit, tie, cuff links, tie pin, new shoes, and socks. He smelled of musky aftershave, which filled the house, masking the stench of cooked cabbage. Now the house had an aroma like the posh perfume counters in the city's fanciest stores.

Dad's hair had been fashionably styled. His ear and nose hair plucked. He looked like a movie star as did Aunt Jane. Both attired in finery I had only ever seen in television movies. I couldn't stop staring as Aunt Jane bossed Dad around and he did exactly as he was told. It was a lesson to see how money and gifts could buy control and obedience.

They'd returned to the house to drop off several shopping bags made of posh dark card, with gold thin rope handles and fancy gold lettering on their sides, displaying the name of the most expensive store in the City. I observed everything about Aunt Jane, as did Michael, Mum said we'd both make good detectives.

The next night, after everyone had gone to bed, I crept downstairs for a glass of water and became alarmed to find a tiny lady creeping around in the kitchen, the moonlight shone on her through the window. I was so startled I almost screamed. It was Aunt Jane, she looked different, shorter without high-heels on, and her wig off. She looked sinister and frail, far removed from the confident woman who had strutted down our path. To my horror, she turned on me, fluttering like a moth; "You're a stupid little girl Hattie," she hissed, as she put her cigarette into her mouth, then grabbed me. Her long fingernails dug deep into my arms. I managed to twist out of her nasty grip and reversed the scenario. I gripped her skinny arms, forcing her to step back as she hissed at me like a snake.

Even though I was eight years old now, I was almost as tall as her and strong. There was no way I would let her hurt me without trying to defend myself. Being on the defensive had become a way of life now and I wasn't putting up with anyone, trying to harm or upset me and my instincts told me that Aunt Jane would try to hurt me whether I fought back or not, so fight back I would, as hard as I bloody well could, just like Dad and Michael taught me to do.

Aunt Jane was about to scream as I dug in deeper with my nails into her flesh. I saw fear in her eyes as I gave her a nasty cow bite. "You hurt me, I hurt you back!" I yelled at her, then added; "I'm a kid, you're a grownup, you're bad, you're evil like your brother," then I let go, and Aunt Jane scurried out of the kitchen like a frightened little mouse before I shouted louder to raise the alarm.

Dad had been right, there were naughty ladies too, his beloved sister was one of them.

Terrified, upset, and shaking, I ran back to Michael's bedroom and hid under the bedclothes of the little camp bed I was to sleep on, while she slept in my sunshine room decorated in sunflower wallpaper with yellow curtains, where she didn't deserve to be. Michael was fast asleep in his tiny, old bed that should have been replaced long ago. His feet stuck out, hovering over the end of the mattress. I tried to stifle my sobs, so as not to wake him.

"She's a nasty, wicked woman; evil, just like Dad," I told Michael, in the kitchen as he bit into a slice of toast the next morning. "We can't trust her, we can't trust him, we have to watch both of them," I warned him. Michael was as furious as I was and agreed to watch her like a hawk.

Mum came into the kitchen; I told her what Aunt Jane did; "I'll keep my eye on her" promised Mum. "What good is that? She's already shaken me and nipped me." I exclaimed. But poor Mum was so downtrodden, her spirit almost broken, she didn't dare speak when Dad and Aunt Jane were around. Telling Aunt Jane off was not on the cards, the repercussions would be enormous, and Dad was waiting for any excuse to hurt Mum. It seemed he was biding his time, then he'd strike when there were no witnesses. For now, he was on his best behavior. He didn't want to upset his sister, whilst she was lavishing him with luxuries, he believed he deserved.

Aunt Jane kept quiet about the incident, but later in the day, she attempted to bribe Michael and me, in the hope I'd keep quiet. She knew full well I'd told Michael what she'd done, but she didn't know I'd already told Mum. She called us into *my* bedroom, which was full of gifts, several tins of hair lacquer, and two wigs perched on a polystyrene wig stand.

"Here you are children, I have gifts for you," she gushed, with a fake smile plastered all over her face. As she glanced at me, she looked nervous and inquisitive...

"You're too late, I've already blabbed," I told her. "Don't you ever touch me again, or I'll tell the police. Oh, and another thing, don't bother trying to bribe us. You can't buy us like you can your brother." Aunt Jane pretended she hadn't heard me, and tried to hand me a doll, I didn't want it. My love of playing with dolls had been taken from me and replaced with self-defense and what I saw as guard duty.

"No thank you, I don't play with dolls," I said, with my arms folded; so, she couldn't push it into my arms. Michael refused to accept a plastic trumpet. "It's like Hattie said, you can't buy us," said Michael.

Then I got my final word in... "He has a real trumpet, he's a musical prodigy, didn't your brother tell you?"

33 UNCLE BARRY ARRIVES

Dad and Aunt Jane were on another shopping trip when Uncle Barry arrived. I'd watched him get out of his burgundy car with a fancy grill, stooping down low as he was so tall and broad. He looked so powerful; he could warn Dad off. Dad would cower in his presence.

Mum rushed out to greet him, she couldn't stop crying with relief, our saviour had arrived. She ushered him into the living room where she poured her heart out to him before he'd even sat down, telling him about the beatings and abuses. "I'm sorry, I have to tell you so quickly, as they might return any minute," she gushed, then continued running through as many accounts of violence as she could, giving him a true picture of our suffering. He could probably see the faded bruises on her cheeks but did not comment. Michael and I sat either side of Mum, all three of us squashed on one chair, holding hands with her, nodding our confirmation, and wincing at what we heard. There were many attacks we knew nothing about. So much pain and suffering. It was a lot to take in. Uncle Barry chewed on his cigar and started to make all the right noises;

"Oh Helen, that's awful, poor you, poor children." For a few minutes, I saw him as our hero. We all seemed hopeful our uncle would help us, that was the reason he came. The feeling of hope soon passed as Dad burst in through the living room door, Uncle Barry jumped up out of the chair, grinning. "Barry... This is a pleasant surprise," said Dad, looking puzzled. He hadn't expected Uncle Barry to be here.

"Hey Lenny, how are you? Long-time, no see," Uncle Barry responded pumping Dad's hand with one hand, whilst patting him on the back with the other. Uncle Barry scanned the room, obviously searching for Aunt Jane. "Why doesn't he punch him?" I asked Michael who looked as dumbfounded as I felt. "He won't do anything," said Michael. "It's like I said, he's only come to see Aunt Jane."

Aunt Jane had dashed upstairs as soon as she'd heard Uncle Barry's loud baritone voice. Five minutes later she slithered into the living-room like a snake, dowsed in expensive seductive perfume, and minty breath freshener. Michael and I watched her as she swooped towards Uncle Barry like a hungry vulture. His face and neck reddened. His breathing became rapid, and a vein twitched in his neck as he gulped. "Just look at him, he's forgotten about us. He came to see her," said Michael. I looked at Aunt Jane; she'd changed from being hard and assertive to absolute mush. It was entertaining, at the same time sickening and very sad. "What's she acting like that for?" I asked Michael.
"She's flirting."
"But he's married," I whispered, shocked. It seemed his having a wife and two children were of no importance to her, and no longer to him. The important ski practice and sightseeing and everything he'd bragged about during Mum's desperate phone call now paled into insignificance.

Aunt Jane sat herself down on the settee, swinging her leg up and down over the other. She wore the most beautiful high-heeled red shoes I'd ever seen. Her toes pointed at Uncle Barry. "Look at the way she's sitting," I whispered, Michael nodded, it was quite an education watching the gestures she used. "She's pointing her toe at him. That means she wants to marry him." I told Michael. I'd learned that from a movie on television. Michael nodded in agreement.

Placing her long cigarette in its elaborate holder, she held it in her hand strangely, gazed at Uncle Barry, then patted the space next to her on the settee, inviting him to sit next to her, flashing her huge Hazel eyes at him. He took the cue without hesitation. "Mind if I join you?" he asked. Of course, she didn't mind, she'd invited him to sit there. He sat down, touching her thigh with his, I could see he didn't need to be so close, there was plenty of room, enough for me to sit there too, but tempted as I was to plonk myself next to him, I watched from my excellent viewpoint, observing everything.

Mum always laughed at the way both Michael and I could read body language, it had become a game to us, one we were superb at, especially for children, we missed nothing, and together analysed everything.

Uncle Barry wriggled his hand in his pocket, delving for his lighter, touching her thigh on the obvious pretence he couldn't find it, with his cigar still lodged in his mouth. I hadn't seen him remove it yet. Aunt Jane stared ahead; pole-faced. It was obvious something was happening. I snapped him out of his search on purpose and offered my help. "Your lighters on the table in front of you. Uncle Barry, can't you see it?" That earned me a glower from both of them and a smile from Michael as if to say I had scored a point. Uncle Barry took the lighter, as Aunt Jane, wrapped her hands around his to suck on the flame to light her cigarette. He lit his cigar and together they sat, gazing at each other through a blanket of smoke, relaying silent, secret messages, wriggling as they sat.

Dad left the room to hunt for his inhaler. His wheezing worsened in the smoker's fog. He turned to look at them as he left, smiling lewdly. We were seeing more of those twisted smiles. The ones that for some reason made me feel sick. I heard him order Mum who was now in the kitchen to put the kettle on and to use the best china. Michael and I shot out of the living room to help her, leaving the two smokers to continue whatever it was they'd started. "What are they doing Mum?" I asked.

"Oh, they're just happy to see each other, don't worry about it. Adults are a little strange sometimes." I knew she wasn't telling the truth. I had an idea.

"Mum, we'll sort the tea and biscuits out," I volunteered, trying to keep down the excitement brewing up within me. I was used to making tea, as Mum always let me help her when the insurance man came around on Friday evenings and the credit collector on Saturday mornings. Everyone got a cup of tea at our house.

I set to work. As soon as the kettle boiled, I put tea leaves in the teapot instead of the latest tea bags. I hid the tea strainer, spat in the hot water, got the chocolate biscuits out instead of the arrowroots, and put them close to the boiling teapot. "This might be funny," I said to Michael, beaming. "It's revenge for not helping Mum and for flirting." We returned to the living room carrying the refreshments on a tray.

We noticed Mum had tried to join in and talk to her brother, but he didn't even notice she was there. She sat alone, snubbed, whilst Aunt Jane and Uncle Barry chatted nonstop as if they were courting. Mum was the reason for his visit, not Aunt Jane.

Dad was still searching for his inhaler, getting madder by the minute, trying hard to suppress his rage. I could hear him losing his temper and banging his feet upstairs, it was obvious he didn't know we could hear him from below.

Putting the tea-laden tray down, I winked at Mum who looked suspicious of me, she knew I'd done something bad, but kept quiet.

With the intent of annoying Aunt Jane and Uncle Barry, I sat down in the tight space next to Uncle Barry when I spotted Dad's inhaler; it was by my side so I pushed it deep into the creases of the settee. Dad would have to keep searching and find another one.

Aunt Jane and Uncle Barry drank their tea, and as they ate the chocolate biscuits, their fingers and teeth became smeared with melted chocolate. Looking at Michael I saw he was almost giving in to laughter. Mum also looked amused but tried to hide her expression. I was furious, emotional, and sorry for Mum and Michael. Uncle Barry was here for bad reasons, not good ones. The initial reason had been ignored.

Interrupting the flirtatious whispering between Uncle Barry and Aunt Jane, I asked, "How are my cousins?" as tears poured down my cheeks because Uncle Barry wasn't helping us. He'd lied to Mum and that upset me a lot. The flirting stopped as they glared at me with hateful eyes which immediately shut me up. I'd just interrupted a moment they shouldn't have been having and reminded him of his family.

Dad bounced back into the room, Uncle Barry and Aunt Jane jumped up out of their tight squeeze, both covered in chocolate. Dad got them a tissue each, then they wiped each other's faces, making a little swab with the tissue. They added a little spittle before they wiped the chocolate off each other, as we sat disgusted.

"We're going now," shouted Dad.

The front door slammed shut as they walked up the path to Dad's car, laughing and chattering.

We three were left behind, deflated. Our only hope had just walked up the path as a traitor, not only to us but to Aunt Laura, Ryan, and Richard. I couldn't stop crying. Like Mum and Michael, I knew we were truly alone, there was no one to help us.

34 GIFTS GALORE

Dad's behaviour had changed dramatically since his sister arrived. He'd gone from being an angry, vile abuser, with vulgar manners, to the perfect gentleman of the house, but only when she was in it, for that, we were thankful.

Aunt Jane appeared to be rich. Her red leather wallet bulged with high-value pound notes which she handed over to Dad on several occasions. We all found it strange to watch them, their performance of giving and receiving was almost ceremonial...

Dad would stand in front of his sister like a child with his hands held out, palms up, as she placed individual notes into his hands. It was as if he was receiving his first pocket money and learning how to count. His sour face lit up with greediness, as his mouth opened and closed, along with his sisters, as they silently counted his daily allowance. We saw fifty-pound notes, twenties, never tens or fives.

"Why has she got to give him so much money, hasn't he got any?" I asked Michael.

"Well he should have lots, as he spends nothing, and he works all the time, I think he's telling her lies so she'll pay for everything."

I asked Mum later, "Do you think she knows Dad has three jobs?"

"I very much doubt it," she replied in disgust. He was keeping the two extra jobs and his freelance work a secret but continued moaning about the main job he'd held for years, the one which had ruined his health, due to the photographic chemicals he'd used on a daily basis, for years. I heard Dad on the phone telling someone he would sue the 'bastards' for causing his bronchitis, but I didn't know what *sue* meant at the time, not until Michael found out and told me.

We could understand Aunt Jane would want to treat Dad and contribute a little money towards her keep, or as a thank you for staying with us, but everything she did was excessive.

Maybe she's guilty because of something bad she did, and now she's paying him to forgive her," Michael suggested. He was super with theories, and I was improving. "Or... maybe she's making up for having a crappy childhood like we're having and buying him stuff to make him forget it all," I suggested.

"Maybe he's blackmailing her," added Michael. We continued guessing. What we did know was; he didn't need her money, not with three jobs, freelance work, and a small contribution to housekeeping. If anyone needed money, it was Mum, Michael, and me. "He's trying to make us look poor, by treating us poor," said Michael.

"Yes!" I shouted, "Katie and Aunt Sarah think we're poor. Dad must have lied and told them that. I hope we aren't like any of them when we're older," I said, disgusted.

Michael looked at me kindly, and reassured me, "Don't worry Hattie, we're nothing like any of them, we never will be."

35 MARKET AND BUMPS

Aunt Jane went out on a day trip with a woman called Audrey and her three children. Audrey was a family friend and had been Dad and Aunt Jane's next-door neighbour for many years.

They must have discussed their plans on the phone for almost an hour. Dad had taken the lock off the phone for his sister saying, "Janie, call anyone you like, don't worry how long you're on or what it costs, just make yourself at home."

Two days later, I saw a photograph of Aunt Jane's day spent with Audrey and her children, two girls and a boy, eating ice cream concoctions, topped with sparklers. in the costly ice cream parlour in town. I knew it was expensive in there, as Michael and I had gazed in through the window once and had seen the prices, each blob of ice cream cost a fortune. All Aunt Jane's guests were laughing and holding balloons. It looked like a birthday celebration. I could see our rejected toys exhibited on the countertop amidst several other gifts looking staged, to display how much the children had been given and how loved they were. The children looked delighted, and I felt happy for them. It was obvious Aunt Jane loved them by how she hugged them. Her smile was enormous like Mr. Evans's. I wondered why she didn't like us, and why we'd hardly seen her smile.

This particular Saturday, Dad stayed in the house, he had no photographs to take. Aunt Jane was out shopping for cashmere sweaters. Her absence meant trouble for Michael and for me.

Mum was grocery shopping, having left at dawn before it got too busy at the market, four miles away. Woe betide her if she spent too much or bought anything Dad didn't like. She'd cycle to her parent's house once she'd finished shopping and spend time with them, helping Gran, as Pop wasn't well.

Dad refused to take Mum to the market in the car, he preferred to watch her struggle on her bike, in all weathers, wearing a rain cape and hood, laden down with heavy provisions to last the week, balancing heavy bags on the handlebars, and a satchel strapped to her back to bring the groceries back to the house. I felt so sorry for her. Yet he'd grovel to Aunt Jane, offering to carry her light, luxury parcels; "Oh, let me help you Janie dear, give me a shout if you need anything else," he'd squeaked in his whiny, subservient voice. "Just phone if you want me to pick you up from anywhere, it's no bother at all." I heard him say, the comparison made me sick. He should have helped Mum.

I'd wanted to go to the market with Mum, but decided it best I stay with Michael. I didn't dare leave him alone with Dad. My instinctive decision proved to be the right one, even though I suffered for having made it.

Michael was in his bedroom, keeping out of Dad's way, I joined him as I didn't want to go near Dad either.

We heard a loud operatic aria blasting out from the living room. It was a record Aunt Jane had bought Dad yesterday, along with a set of Italian language lessons, a gift to help him brush up on his language skills for our trip to Italy.

We could hear Dad screeching along to the opera from Michael's bedroom. He was also making strange thudding sounds; we had no idea what they were.

Michael and I decided to sneak downstairs, with the intent to leave the house via the back door, as we felt vulnerable being in the house alone with him, previously, he'd attacked us, and we were scared.

As we crept past the living room, curiosity drew us to peep in through the jar of the door, to see what the thudding noise was. This proved to be our disastrous mistake.

Both of us stood, frozen to the spot, bearing witness to the weirdest performance we'd ever seen... Dad was dancing and leaping around the room. His facial expressions alternated in time to the music, as his hands conducted an invisible orchestra. The curtains were drawn, the bright central lights switched on.

I fought hard to control my rising giggles that brewed from nerves, fear, and hilarity.

Dad was wearing the dressing gown Mum had bought him in the hope he would keep himself covered and decent in front of us, as he'd recently started walking around with a towel around his waist, which often fell off. I told Mum, and she made it clear to Dad that he should always be dressed when we were around, but he took no notice, he hadn't wanted to remain decent, he wanted us to see him!

After a few minutes, Dad switched the record player off and started singing obscene profanities in the same tune as the opera, making the words fit, building up to a macabre crescendo, then turned to us and smiled.

Michael snapped out of his hypnotic state and dragged me away, sensing something bad was about to happen. Fear enveloped both of us. Frantically, we tried to make our escape. All doors to the outside world were locked. Our only option was to hide, knowing he would come after us.

"You little shits, I'll bloody murder you when I get my hands on you," he threatened, as his game of hunt the children began. We flew out of his sight in a panic and hid.

"Come out ready or not," he called just as he used to when we were playing, but now, it wasn't fun, nor a game. It seemed Dad had an evil plan; to harm and terrify us.

As we hid. I knew I had to keep quiet. Screams were building up inside me. Michael put his shaking hand over my mouth to stifle them. We huddled together, scared out of our wits, in the darkness of the pantry, trying to listen to his whereabouts.

The opera started again; the volume was at its highest level drowning out any movements he made.

Michael and I clung to each other, petrified, buried under piles of junk in the tiny, claustrophobic room. We'd shoved ourselves as far back as we could get, ramming ourselves under the shelf that was covered with old damp coats, plastic bags, stinking canvas shoes, and food that smelled like old cheese and flour. The fear and stench knocked us sick.

It would only be a matter of seconds before Dad came for us. He knew exactly where we were. Dad was toying with us, stretching out our anguish for his own cruel satisfaction and amusement.

We scoured frantically, through the clutter for something to defend ourselves with as he called out our names. Our hands were almost numb as we gripped each other's tightly, our eyes wide open, staring into the darkness of the airless room as Dad began his terrifying game of Hide and Seek.

We popped our heads up slightly from under the stinking heap, to watch him through a tiny gap in the door which he'd recently kicked in. Both of us knew what was coming.

Dad began his theatrics, raging and throwing pots onto the floor in a tantrum, everything on the draining board flew across the kitchen clattering and shattering. He banged a pan wildly against the side of the oven as he sang his murderous lyrics. Obscenities spewed from his repugnant mouth, threatening us in the cruellest ways imaginable. Shaking, we fought to silence our sobs.

He stopped smashing the crockery and ranting, and switched to a soft, playful voice, beckoning us...."Michael, Hattie, come to Daddy," then yelled; "I said bloody well get here now!"

It was another of the most peculiar and terrifying acts we'd ever witnessed. We continued watching through the tiny gap, too scared to blink, transfixed as Dad punched himself on his chest, as if he were Tarzan, his dressing gown open. It wouldn't be long before he took this madness to another level.

Dad knew we were watching him and from where. His head turned as if it was mechanical, pretending to look for us.

My heart palpitated wildly, as he pulled the pantry door open, made a swift grab for Michael. Clutching my brother with one hand, and me with the other, he dragged us out of our hiding place as we screamed for help, and tried to run through the air. Coats and junk trailed behind us as we tried to hold on to anything that would act as an anchor. Huge tins of condensed milk and plum tomatoes crashed down from the shelves behind us as Dad dragged us from our obvious hiding place. He hauled Michael upright and glared at him. There was a split-second opportunity, which Michael didn't miss. He landed Dad with a hard-swift jab straight into Dad's hideous, angry face, fuelled by trepidation and perfect timing, Michael splattered Dad's nose.

Dad seemed shaken; his vision had been impaired. He had no option but to release his grip on Michael and me, to tend to his bleeding nose.

Michael and I made our escape up the stairs into Michael's bedroom, leaving Dad staggering, and whining in the kitchen. We had a two-minute head start on him, but Dad wasn't in a hurry, he had time on his side, we were easy prey, locked in the house with no escape, and no one to help us. "I'll bang your bleeding heads together and knock you little shits senseless," he yelled as he stomped up the stairs after us.

We tried to create a barricade against the door to prevent Dad from getting in. Both of us were terrified. "Help me push the bed up against the door, then push the bookcase up behind it," ordered Michael taking charge, thinking on his feet. We knew we were running out of time.

A minute later, we sat rigid, with our backs against the wall, our feet against the side of the bookcase, the bookcase against the bed, the bed against the door. We hoped we'd done enough to keep Dad out.

Seconds later, Dad was by the door, pushing it, at the same time raging and screaming abuse at us. "Open the sodding door, you little shits," he ordered, as he kicked the wooden panels hard.

We heard him shuffle away, then charge along the landing throwing himself at the door, causing it to move. "Come on kids, let Daddy in," he coaxed, in a sick, yet pleasant, playful voice, as we held hands and stared at the rattling doorknob. My mind was all over the place. I started singing, "Little pigs, little pigs let me in."

"Hattie, stop it!" Michael shouted, he looked at me as if I'd lost my mind, perhaps I had, I was eight years old and scared out of my wits.

Dad wouldn't stop, he continued throwing his weight at the door, determined to burst his way in. We felt the bed move. Inch by inch, backwards we slid, gathering momentum as our legs bent with the force. Then he was in, stood in front of us, gloating. Amusement shone in Dad's eyes as he contemplated how he would knock the shit out of us, just as he'd threatened.

In a rage, he grabbed us by our hair, one of us in each hand, and bumped our heads together, after which he swung us around, almost bouncing us off the walls as if we were rag dolls. Dad pushed, pulled, and shook us, feeding off his rage and our fear, then burst into song, consisting of vile threats, it was his own operatic aria of how he would destroy us, then murder us. We knew the lyrics off by heart after having heard them many times before.

Michael's face had drained of blood, he was terrified, knowing Dad would not hold back on him. Michael was Dad's target. Michael always fought back hard, he was a strong boy, but Dad had taken to sneaking upon him as he did with Mum, like a snake in the grass and then attacked after they were cornered.

Dad flung me across the room, so I couldn't interfere or get in the way. I landed in a heap as I watched on in anguish as Dad pulled Michael's head up with one hand, by his hair. Dad's free hand was clenched into a fist, geared up for a hard punch into the handsome, innocent face of my ten-year-old brother. Wildly, Dad set about pummelling my brother, his son, knocking him sideways, pulling him, in all directions. His eyes had come to life as my brothers looked dead.

I got up, but I was hurt and dazed, yet I threw myself at Dad, trying my best to stop him. My attempts at scratching, biting, and punching out at him were having little to no effect as he was in a frenzy, I couldn't get close. We didn't stand a chance.

Michael seemed to be out cold. He looked like he was asleep on the floor. I was sure he was dead. Murdered by his own father, after having put everything he had into a fast, violent, courageous fight to protect himself, and me from the man who should have loved us.

Dad left the room with a spring in his step. As we lay injured and lost.

36 MUM AND AUNT JANE

I got up from the floor, taking care, so as not to stand on broken glass from a smashed lamp, and covered Michael with a blanket. I held him in my arms, sobbing, unsure of what to do next. He'd tried to save us both, risking his life for me, as I had for him.

Dad had only toyed with me, but he went all out to injure Michael, just like he did with Mum. They fought to save themselves, it was heart-breaking to witness.

Mum arrived on her bike; I heard her call out our names as she walked through the carnage in the kitchen. Her voice verged on the point of hysteria as she called out for us. I didn't answer; not wanting to disturb Michael. He seemed peaceful in my arms, I wasn't sure if he was alive or dead, I had no idea what to do with him other than hold him.

Mum found us, huddled, in the sorriest of states, and dropped to the floor beside us, saying Michael's name. Her face quizzed mine for answers.

After a couple of minutes, my brother came around. I sobbed in relief; I'd thought he had passed. She lifted him up and carried him to his bed and tended to him, he was dizzy, hurt, and bewildered. As Mum checked him over, she found bruises on his tummy, shoulders, back, and face, he'd taken a terrible battering.

Mum felt the bumps on our heads where we had been smashed into each other like symbols.

Aunt Jane returned to the house; she came into the room to look at us. I wondered why? as she didn't like us, maybe she came to gloat. A second later, she waltzed off in her expensive velvet trouser suit, a cigarette stuck to her bottom lip, devoid of emotion. Later, I heard her loud fake voice on the phone arranging happy plans with Audrey, telling her to bring her three wonderful children along; she was taking them out again for another surprise treat. The next day, she and Dad drove off to meet Audrey and her family, they didn't return for three days.

37 GETTING READY FOR ITALY

Soon, the five of us would leave for Italy, our first-ever holiday. We packed what we had for the trip, most of my clothes were threadbare, apart from the two dresses from the jumble sale and my special yellow dress and lemon socks, which I'd packed determined not to associate dad's assault with them any longer. Mum had bought me this lovely yellow dress as a special gift and I would feel beautiful in it, just as she'd intended me to feel.

I somehow understood even at my age, that we had to cling on to good acts, not the bad. We had to get on with life, regardless of how horrendous things were. There was little we could do about any of it, apart from helping fight Dad off, ignoring his rants, and keeping out of his way.

On the day of our departure, our faces were almost clear of bruises and scratches. It had taken several bottles of Witch Hazel to reduce the bruising. Further evidence of the attacks remained hidden under the thick orange-tinted makeup; Mum daubed on our faces.

Mum locked the house, as Michael and I squashed our plastic clothes bags into the car boot around Aunt Jane's five, posh red leather cases.

Packed up like sardines, we sat in the back seats waiting for Dad. Michael sat by one door, me by the other, and Aunt Jane plum in the middle. I would have liked Mum to sit between us, but Aunt Jane demanded she sat there. She had the money, so she made all the decisions.

Dad stood by the car's bonnet turning the starter handle, looking madder with each turn. Once the engine ticked over, he jumped into the driver's seat, and off we went.

"Is that how cars work by winding them up?" I asked. Michael giggled.

"It's not the same as my paper plane which I wind up and let go," he said, eager to explain about engines and mechanics which he loved, but Aunt Jane snarled; "You two, sit back and shut the hell up and bloody well keep still."

Dad smiled at his sister as if he was pleased, she'd taken charge, and he seemed to like the way she'd shut us up so abruptly. Mum looked ready to say something but thought better of it.

"All set Janie, darling?" He asked. Aunt Jane blew out a smoke ring and gave a little nod.

"Off we go then Janie, let's get this show on the road."

38 GRAN AND POP

Before we started the main leg of our ambitious journey, we stopped at Gran and Pop's house to say goodbye. We hadn't seen them for a long time, as we'd been hiding our bruises and distress. Mum said they were too old to be told about the things that went on in our house, they deserved peace at their ages, but it was obvious they had immediately noticed Michael's sorry face when he ran to hug them both.

"Hey, what's all this?" Pop asked as Michael squeezed him with every ounce of energy he had. Pop recognised his need and returned the strong hug.

They asked how the last days at school had been and laughed about my sorry tale about the French horn, telling me not to worry.

Pop said I would be good at art; it was in our genes. All Mum's side of the family were professional artists, and I was discovering I was artistic too.

Gran and Pop were proud to learn of Michael's musical progress and Michael promised to play his trumpet for them on our return.

Before we left, they gave Michael and me pads of paper and pencils. "If you have time, draw your adventures for us, so we know what you saw and where you went." Pop suggested, encouragingly. Then Gran scurried out of the room and returned with her arms full of bags and passed them over to all of us. The bags were full of homemade cakes, sandwiches, and bottles of ginger ale to keep us satiated until we got to Dover. Touched, I couldn't help but cry because of their kindness.

"What's up Hattie?" asked Gran.

"I love you both; I'll miss you so much," I told her. Gran held me close and kissed my forehead.

"You are both so kind to us," I said.

"You stay strong, Hattie," she said. I realised she knew bad things were happening to us. Gran was the wisest woman in the world and Pop was the wisest man, I'd noticed his concerned expression hadn't left his face, as he stared daggers at Dad still sitting in the car.

Gran's hug transferred energy and strength into me, like an electric charge. It seemed pop had passed the same charge to Michael.

Our grandparents were soulmates who adored each other, I'd never seen them look miserable, or heard them say anything nasty.

Pop was an inventor and an artist; he could make and fix anything. He'd made Gran an ornamental fountain out of concrete and an old barrel that looked like those in magazines, which showed stately homes and expensive houses.

He'd made concrete rabbits using jelly molds and painted them to look realistic. Pop would hide them in the garden under bushes and plants, it was our job to find them. Whoever found the most rabbits won a prize, usually a packet of crisps he'd made with a pinch of salt wrapped in blue paper, which we searched for merrily, through the bursting brown bag, overloaded with crisps. We were supposed to eat only a quarter to a half of the bag, the remaining crisps were to be saved until the next day, but we couldn't stop eating them once we'd started.

My favourite game was croquet which Pop made on his fretsaw machine, using scraps of wood and concrete. Michael liked the archery set best. Pop taught us how to use them, saying... "If you have patience and you practice often, then you can achieve anything you set your heart on." This spurred us on to improve at the games in his garden and lessons at school.

Not only did he give us words of wisdom from his own experience, but he showed us how to make things, using layman's terms, until we knew how to achieve a satisfactory result. Our self-pride and confidence soared after each visit.

Pop taught me how to write in copperplate and other styles of lettering, I was proficient for a child, but I knew I'd have to practice a lot and I did with lettering; I would spend my spare time copying various styles until they were as close to perfect as I could get them, Michael said he wasn't surprised I was good at copying because I'd always been a copycat.

Our grandparents had little money, but everything they had was beautiful and made with skills which they'd taught themselves. "We have to make things better, not worse," Pop would say. He was the opposite of Dad as Dad liked to make good things bad. Mum must have missed this world so much.

It was almost time to go. Pop placed one of his prize roses in my hair and tweaked my cheeks, making me smile. "Thanks, Pop," I said, gazing at him for a long time, taking in every detail of his kind, wrinkled face, with the bluest of eyes, that could see into souls. I wanted to take his vision with me on the journey. How I wished Dad had been like him.

Gran came towards me, with her arms outstretched for a cuddle, I jumped into them, loving her warm hug which I needed more than ever.

"I love you, Gran," I told her.

"And I love you too Hattie, very much," she said.

I became emotional as she said, "We are always here for you, Michael, and your Mum. If you need us, you must call." I bit my lip to stop myself from sobbing and nodded. My throat burned, I couldn't swallow, as she seemed to know we were suffering at the hands of Dad, knowing she cared so much and that she knew, touched me.

We left, waving through the windows of the car, Pop and Gran waved back, their expressions looked sad, even though they smiled. They continued waving until we were out of sight.

Dad and Aunt Jane had stayed in the car during our rushed visit. We drove along the dual carriageway, then the old car stalled. Dad got out, exasperated because he had to turn the starting handle again. Ten minutes later, we drove away.

Michael and I sat in silence, squashed against Aunt Jane on the back seat, the windows had steamed up with condensation mixed with cigarette smoke, so we couldn't even see out clearly.

39 DOVER TO CALAIS

We arrived at Dover. Soon we would board the huge Ferry to Calais. Mum burst into a song about the white cliffs of Dover. We knew it too, so joined in, happy our holiday was about to start. Dad snapped; "Shut it," as Mum recoiled in her seat.

Michael and I watched the ferries, they were bigger than we'd imagined. We saw so many boats, yachts, and cruise liners, never having seen anything like them before. Hundreds of cars, coaches, trucks, and motorbikes waited in long queues to board the same ferry as us. Horns never stopped honking. Everybody rushed to get on board in what seemed like chaos. It was thrilling.

Dad said we had to stay inside the car for most of the journey, he only allowed us out of the car to go to the bathroom.

"This holiday is horrible, I hate it," I whispered to Michael, as we stood outside the car for a few moments, to get our circulation back and stretch our cramped limbs.

"So, do I, Hattie."

"Aunt Jane scares me, she's evil," I told Michael, nodding towards her. He agreed.

"Have you got your itching powder with you?" Asked Michael.

"Yes, I do, I always carry it," I answered, feeling happier.

"Don't lose it whatever you do!" he stressed.

"Don't worry Michael, I won't," I responded tapping my head with my hand, implying wig. We laughed.

"Don't you two upset anyone," Mum warned us, she'd noticed we were up to something. We got back inside the car and sat in place for ages, uncomfortable, and miserable, under the evil eye of Dad and his cruel sister.

After a while, we took a natural break in the ferry bathroom before disembarking.

The restrooms were full. Dozens of people queued up along the deck. Aunt Jane refused to go; she didn't dare move as the swaying motion of the ferry made her seasick. She'd turned a horrible shade of green. Michael told me she would puke soon. We made bets on how long it would take her before she threw up all over the place.

The bathroom was disgusting. Urine overflowed from the toilet basins and flooded the deck. We watched the massive puddle change direction as the ferry moved with the tide.

We saw people rush towards the bathrooms, shouting for a cubicle with great urgency because they were seasick, just like Aunt Jane.

Michael and I stood in the bathroom queue for ages, waiting for our turn. Our white gym shoes were soaked from the river of yellow putrid urine which continued flooding every time someone pulled the toilet chain. I heard someone say the toilets were blocked.

The car would stink even more once we got back inside, as our shoes were the only ones we had, we couldn't throw them away, so the smell had to come with us.

On our return to the car, we saw Aunt Jane standing next to it, vomit all down the front of her beautiful clothes. Dad stood on the other side of the car struggling to breathe. His sister's smoke had affected him, but he said nothing. He didn't dare upset her as she was paying for this trip of a lifetime, one which we felt scared of talking or laughing on.

It looked like Dad needed help, but we turned the other way, he deserved none from us.

I looked at Aunt Jane, she looked horrific. Against her wishes, she needed to throw up again. "Just going to the bathroom," she mumbled, then sped off, but didn't make it, we saw her come to a standstill, her head went down. Seconds later she rushed towards the bathrooms. I struggled to hide my laughter, as did Michael.

We hadn't warned her how disgusting it was, or how long the queue was as we were being seen and not heard, just as we'd been told. They couldn't have it both ways.

When Aunt Jane returned, she looked even ghastlier. Her pretty blouse soaked as she'd been sick down its front again. Her burnt coffee-coloured nylons and classy shoes were drenched in urine and vomit.

She'd had to paddle through the disgusting quagmire, just like we had, and she stank to high heavens, just like us.

"I never expected that," she moaned in disgust. Michael and I sniggered.

An hour later we disembarked. Dad drove down the ramp at a snail's pace, and turned onto the exit road from the port, after waiting to be waved on by officials.

We started our journey through Calais and deeper into France, hoping Dad would drive through Paris as we had heard so much about it and seen films showing the Eiffel Tower. As soon as one of us asked if we could see it, Dad shouted; "No you sodding well can't."

We were filthy, the car stank, we hadn't freshened up in hours and we needed to get out of the car again to get our circulation back and cough out the smoke we'd been inhaling. Mum made the mistake of asking if we could book into a motel to sort ourselves out. Dad snarled; "If you think I'm paying for a bloody motel, you've got another bloody think coming." Aunt Jane's treat didn't include accommodation.

"We'll sleep in the car and if you don't like it, then bloody well get out," he snarled. The hard, sweaty seats which didn't recline were our beds for the four nights it took to get to Taranto.

We drove for miles, sat in filth, eating sandwiches Gran and pop had given us, which were now stale and dry. The fizzy drinks were flat, but they had to be rationed between us. We wouldn't get anything else.

Dad knew people everywhere. He spoke French well. Michael and I didn't understand a word he said, though Mum did and didn't look too pleased with him, especially when we were in the house of Maria and Rosa in Switzerland. Both women gushed all over Dad. It seemed they knew him well, from a life he'd had before, one we knew nothing about.

They seemed like lovely people and gave us a bar of chocolate. Dad grabbed the huge slab, broke off one square each for Michael and myself, then ate the rest, once back in the car, and out of sight.

40 CIGARETTE BURNS

It was purgatory sitting in the back of the car with Aunt Jane in the middle of Michael and me. She was unfriendly and cruel. She burned me twice, with her lit cigarette all because I'd had pins and needles from sitting still for hours, so wriggled.

Aunt Jane had leaned in close to me, and whispered, "Sit still and keep quiet," as she positioned her cigarette next to my arm to ensure I felt its heat. A second later, she jabbed it onto the flesh of my left arm; "Don't say a word or I'll do it again," she threatened under her stinking, tobacco breath.

I opened my mouth to raise the alarm as she burned me again with the hot end which she'd puffed on to make even hotter. I stifled my screams, so as not to set Dad off again as he'd already threatened to crash the car. Both of them petrified me.

Aunt Jane continued moving her hand which held the cigarette close to my arm. I saw her glare at me from the corner of her eye, like an iguana with heavy lids. The lit cigarette was a constant warning for me to sit still and keep quiet, otherwise, my flesh would meet its cruel end a third time.

Other times she would jab me hard with her elbow, pretending the motion of the car made her do it. I knew I should tell, but if I did, Dad would take her side and he'd drive faster to scare us. He'd often put his foot down on the accelerator, then swerved as we drove along crowded streets and over the Alps. We sat terrified.

Sometimes, I would sit curled up against the car door, tempted to open it, and jump out, wanting to run, far away from these two cruel bullies who should have loved us, but then Mum and Michael would be alone with them, so I couldn't do it.

Michael knew she was being nasty to me. He heard her tell me I was horrible, the worse girl she'd ever known, but she didn't know me and I didn't care what she thought.

Michael tried to hold my hand over the back of the seat, behind Aunt Jane's head; to let me know I wasn't alone, but I didn't dare move to take it.

Mum would periodically ask if everything was all right. Aunt Jane would answer on our behalf with lies, "Yes Helen, everything's good in the back," she was lying with fake sincerity, it wasn't fine at all, and it was all her fault and Dad's.

I looked through the front window as we drove through Switzerland. It was gorgeous. I'd seen chocolate boxes in the sweet shop, with pictures of the Alps on the lid. To see them in reality, was breath-taking.

We pulled into a layby to finish the dry sandwiches which were showing signs of mould; we had to scrape it off and eat them.

Michael and I got out of the car and ran up and down the mountainside, out of Dad's earshot in case he yelled for us to get back in the car. We rolled down the steep hills on our sides, laughing and enjoying the few minutes of freedom we had.

We discussed the bad behaviour of Dad and his sister and promised each other we would stay strong and not let them destroy us.

After our serious discussion, we followed the lizards as they ran through the grass. We drank water from the waterfalls, splashing our faces and hair to freshen up. I placed my burnt arm under a small waterfall for instant relief, then put my cardigan back on to hide the two ugly burns.

Mum found us. She kissed and cuddled us, and apologized for the unpleasant trip, though it wasn't her fault. She told us to stay brave and strong. Then the happy moment was ruined as we heard Dad shout; "Get back in the bleeding car!"

41 WE ARRIVED IN TARANTO

We arrived in Taranto. Our horrendous journey came to an abrupt halt, in the middle of the most chaotic city we'd ever been in. We heard car horns honking, people playfully shouting, others yelling at drivers for what I guessed was bad driving.

Dozens of mopeds which Michael told me were Vespers dodged between the traffic. The area seemed alive with excitement. I felt the adrenaline brewing up inside me, and relief when Mum pointed out the 'Taranto' sign.

We were almost at our destination. We'd found the city, now we needed to find the apartment.

Dad told us to get out of the car; the putrid stench came with us. My brother and I stood on the pavement, observing our new surroundings. I felt overwhelmed with the ambiance, as I watched people greet each other as they passed by, they kissed and hugged each other. Everyone looked so happy.

There were hundreds of apartments with balconies, each one laden with beautiful flowers, cascading to the lower levels in colours I'd never seen.

We could still hear the wonderful sound of grasshoppers, and the sound of the street cleaner's small carts, whizzing along the roadsides, cleaning up from the night before. Michael and I loved every sight and sound.

People walked past us, saying Buongiorno, genuinely happy to greet us, we felt welcome. Both Michael and I were in awe. "They don't know us," I said to Michael, thrilled someone had spoken to us. I thought we were invisible and didn't matter. That feeling passed, and I smiled again as we watched parents playfully swing their children up into the air as the little ones squealed with delight.

Couples walked along the beautiful tree-lined street where we parked, laughing and chatting, holding hands. They looked like they were in love, stopping for an occasional sweet kiss. I felt happy for them, yet overwhelmed with sadness for Michael, Mum, and myself. "I wish we could be happy like them," I whispered to Michael. He squeezed my hand in empathy. My eyes filled with tears as a lump of sadness lodged in my throat.

42 PIZZA PARLOUR

"That's enough sodding gawping. Get back in the bloody car and look for the apartment, we could be miles away," Dad yelled at us, ignoring the horrified faces of the people who witnessed his outburst.

We jumped back into our seats; fear had trained us well, and drove around for hours searching for Aunt Clelia's apartment, but which one? There were thousands of identical apartment blocks. Dad hadn't given us the address, nor a landmark to look for.

We didn't dare tell him he'd missed the most important information, so we pretended to look for it. Our noses were glued against the car windows, taking in the most glorious views and watching the happy people bustling around the city.

"Can you see it yet?" He shouted, every few seconds.

"No," Michael and I responded in unison. I struggled with my giggles as this was ridiculously funny. It was Dad's own fault.

Dad became angrier by the minute as he drove around in circles. Aunt Jane hadn't glanced through the window once to help with the search, only stared ahead, puffing out smoke.

Mum was eager to point out things of interest to us but didn't dare say anything. She nodded her head to indicate there was something of interest for us to look at. We caught on to her actions and missed nothing. Mum was like us, enthusiastic, thrilled, and eager to explore, but had to keep her excitement contained, otherwise she'd feel the back of Dad's hand. He'd already hit her three times, for no reason.

Whilst in the car Mum remained deadpan and rigid. The only time we saw her move was when we stopped for natural breaks and when she put her hand out of the window to signal cars to pass us by, as we slowed down, which we did often. I felt so sad for her.

We pulled up next to an apartment block at the side of a large busy Junction. Dad got out of the car looking flummoxed. He buzzed a number on a copper-coloured plate to an apartment block that had over twenty buttons, then spoke into an intercom.

Several minutes later, a smart, petite lady in a tweed suit and a severe bun in her hair came to greet us. It was Aunt Clelia. She wasn't a family member; I wondered why we should call her Aunt.

We watched as Aunt Clelia gushed over Dad, stroking his face as if he was a little child, "Oh Leonardo, Leonardo," she uttered, as tears streamed down her face.

She acknowledged Mum, but Dad told her to stay in the bloody car, we guessed he meant us too.

Aunt Jane got out of the car, clambering over poor Michael, standing on his feet with her high-heels. I saw he was in pain, but she didn't care.

Ten minutes later we were let out of the car and we followed the adults into the large apartment block.

Squashing into the small lift we went up to floor number eight. I wondered what would happen if Dad broke wind like he had all the way here, then I had a problem trying not to laugh.

We got out of the lift as Aunt Jane continued fawning all over this tiny lady, laughing and hugging her as if she was the most important woman in the world.

Mum pulled Michael and me close, cuddling us as she whispered; "Don't worry, we will have fun!"

Aunt Clelia opened the apartment door and ushered us into the bedroom we were to share for the next three weeks with Aunt

Jane. The overwhelming smell of mothballs hit me full-on and made me cough. The room was dark, closed in by dark wooden shutters, making it feel like I imagined prison to feel. Michael opened a shutter slightly that hadn't been fastened down. We both peeped out to see hundreds of other apartments, all back to back, it all looked so exciting, we would have liked to sit on the balcony and study each apartment, look at the flowers, the washing hanging down and the children playing, but Aunt Jane quickly closed the shutters.

Mum and Dad had been taken to see their room. Ours had three single narrow beds. Aunt Jane, chose the middle one, no doubt to prevent Michael and me from chatting.

We stood in the bedroom watching Aunt Jane take out her red leather wallet from her matching bag. She opened it, displaying a thick wad of money. To our surprise, she handed Michael several high-numbered notes.

"Here you are ya little shits, clear off, and don't bother coming back till later, ten o'clock will do it," she snarled.

I felt myself rise to protest, but Michael tugged my arm to stop me. He was a lot calmer than me; he thought things through and didn't overreact. "Hattie, let's go, we're free now, I'll look after you," he promised in a whisper.

As we opened the door to leave the apartment, ready to explore the freedom of the city, I glimpsed Aunt Jane in the hallway mirror. Our bedroom door was in line with the mirror, so I could see her.

I told Michael to hide with me behind the coat stand whilst we watched her, and I plotted. She took her wig off and placed it on her special stand on top of the dresser, then swapped it for an identical one from her case. Her real hair looked like someone had glued it to her head with several cans of lacquer.

She changed her high heel shoes for another pair, then practiced smiling in the dressing-table mirror. Happy with her look, she disappeared back to Aunt Clelia.

I fidgeted in my pocket, and sneaked back into the bedroom, took the wig off the stand and sprinkled itching powder inside, then took the shoes and sprinkled it in those too. "Serves you right," I whispered to no one.

"What are you doing? Come on Hattie hurry up," urged Michael, eager to go. I completed my mission, then we left. It was a relief to get out of there; it felt like we were escaping a prison sentence. Our adventures were about to begin.

Instead of using the lift, we ran down the eight flights of stairs, laughing and joking all the way down, leaping off several steps at a time, racing to see who could get down to the ground floor first. Both of us were glad to use up energy. We'd been cooped up for days, now we were free.

Once outside the old apartment building, we stood around the corner, out of sight. Michael and I needed to decide what to do next. Crowds of people skirted around us, so as not to bump us, that made me cry, as Dad had bumped into us so many times, to hurt us on purpose.

"Hattie stop it," Michael whispered, as he saw me becoming emotional. "Come on Hattie, pull yourself together, you're a very strong little girl, and we will have adventures, we're free now," he said.

A pretty lady passed by us, but returned to stroke my hair. She must have noticed I was upset and smiled; I smiled back, then she continued walking, taking a final glance at Michael and me before disappearing around the corner.

Suddenly, we were part of the Taranto scene. I blew my nose, then whispered in Michael's ear; "I've put itching powder in her wig and her shoes. She's been horrible to us so I'm being horrible to her." He laughed.

I felt happy having put my powder to such good use. "She'll scratch herself to bits later," I chuckled.

"If she finds out what you've done, she'll be even nastier to you, and Dad will leather you, so you have to be very careful Hattie," Michael warned me.

"She's already been nasty, it's my turn now," I said. "Anyway, we can say we saw fleas in the apartment when she scratches." We roared with laughter, we had an excuse and we'd scratch when Aunt Jane did.

We contemplated our next move, both overwhelmed. Knowing we were unwanted, abandoned, lost, and hopeless.

"We need to make sure we can find our way back to the apartment," said Michael taking charge in a mature, caring manner. It was then I realised, why Mum trusted him so much.

I didn't know my way around the massive council estate we lived on, so I wondered how we would ever find our way around this huge city. We couldn't speak Italian and had no sense of direction. It would be a daunting challenge for us. Michael said to think of it as a confidence-building exercise, which would strengthen us. I liked that thought and felt stronger immediately.

Michael looked at me, concerned; "Hattie, you know this is neglect, right? We shouldn't be here on our own like this." I hadn't realised, I was eight years old, Michael was only ten. I didn't know much, but I was learning, albeit too fast.

"At least we're away from the bully and his wicked sister. If they can't find us, it's their fault, but why is Mum allowing all this neglect?" I asked.

"Have you seen how frightened she is?" Asked Michael, I nodded.

"He'll do something bad if she doesn't do as he tells her. He wants us out of the way, so we have no choice," said Michael.

"What will he do to her?" I asked, feeling myself tremble, things were already bad.

"It will be something worse than we know, otherwise she would have reported him to the police ages ago. Mum's not weak, she's scared stiff, and trapped. We can't help her, we must survive out here, and I have to look after you." Michael said.

"Let's try our best to enjoy ourselves, while we're away from him, we can't go back, so there's nothing we can do," said Michael.

Michael wrote our new Italian address on the paper that Gran and Pop gave us and warned me; "We don't talk to anyone, only if we get lost. You and I stay together and you don't let go of my hand. I can't lose you, Hattie, you're still a little girl, even though you don't think so," he told me. For the first time in ages, I felt safe.

"If we get split up, go into a shop and tell the shopkeeper the name of the apartment that's written on the paper. Keep the paper in your pocket, I'll keep the other in mine."

We set about exploring, finding our way, familiarising ourselves with block after block of tall apartments, writing, and drawing landmarks to ensure our safe return to the apartment, like Hansel and Gretel.

Fortunately, we found a pizza parlour, which we'd smelled a block away. The aroma of garlic and oregano drew us up to the window. We'd never seen pizzas before. Both of us were drooling and fascinated as we peered in, watching men in chefs' hats and aprons toss dough over their hands like jugglers.

They'd stretch the dough bases, put them onto long shovels, cover them with various ingredients, and push them into three huge ovens, not long after, they would pull out the most incredible-looking food imaginable.

The scene fascinated us as we dithered over how much one pizza would cost, hoping we had enough Lira.

A man stood behind the counter spotted us, and knocked on the window, gesturing for us to enter. He could tell we couldn't speak Italian and smiled when I pointed to a picture of a pizza, hung on the wall, making it known we would like one. Michael showed the man our lira, he took a paper note from us, gave Michael change, then escorted us to a table covered in a red and white checked tablecloth, with a candle in a bottle, covered in melted wax. He brought us two glasses of milk, then stood back, smiling at us.

"I think he's given them to us," said Michael. We smiled, and gulped down the refreshing cold milk, both of us parched. We liked him. Michael nodded his thanks, the man smiled again, then pointed to his name badge on his red shirt, the same colour as the menus, it read; Mario.

Michael pointed and said, "Hattie," then to himself, "Michael," we shook hands. Now we had a friend called Mario in Taranto and were about to eat pizza for the first time in our lives. At last, we'd found happiness.

Mario brought out two cloth napkins, shook them, and tied them around our necks, chatting to us in the most wonderful language, that sounded musical and fast. It all seemed like a dream.

Mario disappeared for a moment. He returned, carrying the most enormous pizza on a silver platter, perched on top of his palm, high above his head. We loved this. He cut into the pizza and placed a large slice on our plates, picked up a large pepper pot, and sprinkled pepper all over the top of our pizza slices.

Mario smiled as we tucked in, devouring the best food we'd ever tasted until our tummies bulged, and we were happier than we'd ever been. From then on, we returned every evening and never figured out how much the pizzas cost, as our lira amount hadn't declined.

We arrived at the pizza parlour at eight-thirty, most evenings, after our adventures in the city. We felt safe and happy there.

When Mario had a few minutes spare, he'd try to teach us Italian. He showed us photographs of his children; they looked as if they were similar in age to us. They looked smart and happy, stood beside a beautiful lady. I looked closer; she looked familiar. I remembered her; she was the lady who'd stroked my hair when I cried the day we arrived. I wondered if she had told Mario about us and asked him to look out for us.

Mario must have told the staff about the two scruffy, unaccompanied children his wife had spotted, who now came for evening pizza, and asked him to keep an eye on us. I wondered how many people knew about us, and what did they think about us being dumped.

After it became clear Michael, and I would eat there every evening, at the same time, Mario put a card on a table with Michael and Hattie printed on it. Our table now was reserved and positioned close to the kitchen where he and his staff could keep an eye on us.

If the parlour was too busy for us to sit there, then we'd have our pizza in the tiny staff room, where the staff would make us fancy ice creams, similar to those which Aunt Jane had bought for Audrey's children.

Every evening we returned to the apartment at ten o'clock. No one asked where we'd been or what we'd been doing. Mum would glance at us, in response, we'd nod to let her know we were all right. We wished we could run-up to her and tell her about our new friend, the incredible pizzas, how we spent our days, and find out how she'd been, but we had to go to our room and keep quiet.

Dad and his sister hadn't spoken to us since she gave us the lira, she and Dad didn't care if we came back or not.

I suggested to Michael we hide somewhere for two nights, to see if they worried, but he said it seemed too risky and might backfire on us.

We stayed in Taranto for two weeks. Michael and I were left to our own devices for most of the time. We'd become familiar with our new surroundings and made friends with the local children, who'd taught us snippets of Italian. In return, we'd taught them English phrases.

We had more fun than we'd ever experienced, jumping in and out of fountains, playing tag around small orange groves, and catching lizards in the central park.

The children's parents would invite us to picnics of ciabatta sandwiches, and fresh orange juice, accepting us as friends, which placed us in awe. We were in a different world far removed from the one we knew.

On rare occasions, Mum would come out to be with us. We were at our happiest then, watching her laugh, run and play. She had the metabolism of a teenager. Our new friends adored her too. They'd never seen an older mother run as fast as Mum.

At curfew time, ten o'clock, we had to go back to the apartment, Mum's face changed to one of gloom. "Why are you so sad Mum, what's happening in the apartment?" Michael asked, we needed to know, as it concerned us. "Nothing for you two to worry about," she answered. We didn't believe her.

Our holiday ended too quickly. It was time to make our arduous return journey to our gloomy house.

Realising we had only minutes to spare, Michael, and I ran as fast as we could, to say our goodbyes to Mario and thank him for being our friend and protector. He looked pleased to see us as we entered the parlour. Michael put out his hand to shake Mario's, they shook, then Mario pulled him into his arms and gave him a very much needed fatherly hug, as if he'd known all along something was wrong in our lives. He knew Michael had been looking after me though Michael also needed looking after.

I felt myself becoming emotional. Mario turned his attention towards me, tweaked my apple cheeks, and gave me a gentle hug. He said something I didn't understand, but it made me cry.

I didn't want to leave this wonderful place. Michael and I had been made welcome here and treated with kindness and respect; we had felt wanted.

We heard a car screech to a halt outside the parlour, then impatient honking. Dad had tracked us down and raced here and parked by our secret place. How did he know where to find us?

The feeling of dread returned, as we watched Aunt Jane open the door for us to get in. Dad's head jutted out of the window on his side of the car, his arm gesticulating wildly, for us to hurry up. "Get in the bloody car," he yelled at the top of his voice as passers-by glared at him for being so nasty.

We took one last look at our friend, who stood by the open door, frowning and staring at Dad as if he wanted to punch him, then looked at us as we climbed into the back of the car.

We watched Mario wave to us until we could see him no longer. Dad sat angry, behind the wheel of his car. His ghoulish sister continued smoking. Mum sat stock still in the passenger seat.

Michael and I shed tears as we drove away, from the best time of our childhoods. Gazing through the window we bid our farewells to the happy times we'd had, dreading what we were driving towards.

43 HOMEWARD BOUND

The return journey through Italy, Switzerland, and France to England was horrendous. Dad's driving became more erratic and faster. It seemed we were in a rush to get back.

We drove through the night, with few stops, Dad was furious, for reasons only he knew, showing his displeasure by swearing and swerving on steep, bends on the Alps.

Dad sang how he would drive the whole bloody lot of us over the edge of the mountains. His lyrics became explicit, and profane, detailing our demise. When I looked at Aunt Jane, for her reaction to his disgusting outburst, she didn't have one; she looked as if everything was normal.

Several times Dad swerved to avoid oncoming traffic. Those we swerved past honked their car horns and shouted at us. Others gesticulated angrily through their windows.

After hours of unnecessary stress and fear, we arrived back to our council estate, tired and upset by the horrid journey, worried about what lay ahead. Our old Humber Hawk hissed and clanked to a standstill by our green gate.

Seeing the depressing houses again through the car window made me sad. There were no hanging baskets with flowers in, and no bright whitewashed houses only dull brick ones with unkempt gardens. Our road was devoid of people filling up water jugs from communal fonts. Nobody gathered to laugh and chat or dance to lively music from someone's radio from a balcony above. Our estate was depressing, with miserable people who gossiped and shouted. I hated it.

Suddenly, to our absolute surprise and delight, a dozen kids from our road surrounded the car, bouncing up and down on the steaming hot bonnet. Two kids squashed and slid their dirty faces all over the windows, slobbering on the glass.

The neighbourhood kids had been waiting upon our arrival for hours, eager to learn all about "Abroad." It overwhelmed us to receive such a greeting.

Dad flew out from his side of the car, looking furious; "Clear off, ya little bastards, you've messed the bleeding windows up," he snarled. No one took a blind bit of notice of him. They pounced on Michael and me, asking a million questions all at once, as we attempted to climb from the rear of the car. Two of them yanked at our arms, dragging us out by our sleeves, much to Aunt Jane's horror.

In 1968 no one we knew had ever been on holiday, especially not to three different countries all in one go. We had only ever had a day trip to the beach before, and that was considered a great treat.

Dana Ward said we were a very adventurous, lucky family for having travelled so far. She got upset when we told her we'd been abandoned in the city and it hadn't been a holiday, but some kind of weird mission. She'd looked astonished and thought we were absolute heroes to have survived and wanted to hear more.

I found it disgusting that we'd had to rely on a stranger to look after us, one who'd become our friend, one who took it upon himself to ensure we remained safe. Perhaps we reminded him of his own children.

We'd been fortunate to meet Mario, he had been the best part of our holiday, thanks to him, we learned that not all people were bad. He'd been caring and kind, without ulterior motives, he gave us hope for the future. Michael and I would never forget him.

We didn't know why we had driven all the way to Italy; we could only guess Dad had gone visiting his past, and some women we met, were perhaps girlfriends from his previous life, hence all the mutual gushing and flushed faces.

Mum never told us what she went through, whilst stuck in the apartment with Dad and his sister. We knew it must have been something bad. She'd looked so sad and afraid every time we saw her. I swore I would find out even if it took a lifetime.

44 AUNT JANE LEAVES

Aunt Jane left for New York two days after we returned, that day couldn't have come around quick enough.

"Enjoy your itchy wigs," I said, as I peeped through my bedroom window, watching to make sure she left and looking for signs of scratching. I had given all her wigs a final top-up of powder, as a warning to behave herself.

"See you next year Lenny darling, thank you so much, sweetie, I'll call you when I get to the apartment," she hollered through the open taxi window, as Dad waved her off. "Cheerio Janie, thanks for everything, I'll wait for your call," he shouted back to her, waving his white handkerchief to bid her farewell.

"Oh no, she's coming next year," I warned Michael, who'd just walked into my room. We watched as the taxi drove off, through the net curtains which had turned yellow from her having smoked in there.

I noticed she'd left a wig behind.

"It won't be long until the itching powder in the one on her head becomes itchy," I laughed, so pleased with myself that I danced and jumped on my little bed with glee.

"Did you put it in anything else?" asked Michael.

"What do you think? Of course, I put it in her shoes, wigs, and her lovely new undies."

Tears streamed down my face as I giggled. We continued bouncing on the bed, scratching our heads, and flaring our nostrils like Aunt Jane did when angry, laughing at me being such a daredevil and not missing out on an opportunity.

Justifying myself, I pointed out; "It's a tiny price for cigarette burns." Michael looked sad and agreed. We knew it would take more than a sprinkling of itching powder to stop a woman from being nasty, one whose nature was pure evil, just like her brother's.

45 NORMAN

Dad hadn't said a word to us since Aunt Jane left. We hadn't spoken to him either. One day, out of the blue, I heard him say to Mum; "I have to visit my father, he's much worse." He wanted one of us to go with him. Michael had trumpet practice, so I needed to go.

The horror stories I heard about him scared me. I'd only ever seen Grandad Norman once, from a distance, dressed up in a long black coat and a bowler hat, he looked exactly like Scrooge. Michael said he looked like the Grim Reaper.

After trying to wriggle my way out of going, for at least ten minutes, Dad lost patience and yelled at me; "Hattie, get in the bloody car and stop being so bloody awkward, you're a pain in the neck."

Once I'd climbed into the car, I refused to talk or look at Dad. I stared through the side window, keeping myself as far away from him as possible. Knowing I'd never forgive him for what he had done to us.

"Okay, you little bitch, have it your own bloody way, I won't talk to you, but you'd better bloody well behave yourself," he hissed as I sat fuming, fighting back the urge to respond. My eyes burned with tears I didn't want him to see. I behaved myself well, we all did, it was he who misbehaved.

We arrived at a depressing row of houses, set in the middle of one of the oldest council estates in the city. All the houses looked the same, devoid of colour. Every window had dirty net curtains tied back, and an aspidistra placed on each windowsill.

The house we were going to, looked foreboding and evil, I dreaded going in. Dad tapped on the front door. A woman whom I knew to be Audrey let us in, whispering to Dad, "I don't think he'll last much longer."

This house was the most stomach-churning building I'd ever been in, even worse than ours. The hallway was knee-deep in rubbish, it stank of stale urine, and worse. We squeezed past the heavy wooden furniture and mountains of clutter that filled the entire hallway.

There were steep stairs leading to the bedrooms, but from what I saw, it looked too spooky for me to run up and nose around as I did at Gran and Pop's house. Michael would love it. This would be the perfect location for him to scare the heck out of me.

Black mould covered the walls. One flickering bare bulb hung from the nicotine-stained ceiling by a shredded cable. Dust half an inch thick sat on top of every surface, never to have been disturbed. I sniffed and sneezed as the dust affected my allergy.

Gripping my own hands, for self-comfort, we walked to the back room where Norman lay, 'dying.' I stayed hidden behind Dad.

I didn't want anything to do with this man; he wasn't worthy to be my Grandad, not after what I'd heard, that's why I called him Norman..., he'd been horrible to Grandma Fay, he'd killed her will to live. She'd preferred death to life with him. He'd treated her so bad for years, tormenting, bullying, and insulting her, as Dad did to Mum.

Grandma Fay died of a heart attack one week after Norman broke her arm. He'd snapped it almost in half. A clean break, halfway through the bone, after which he'd wrenched open her tiny clenched fist as she clung to her step cleaning money.

She'd needed that money to feed their children, and he'd wanted to gamble it away on the dog track, where he'd gone every night to lose everything they had.

Grandma Fay died a week later, just a few days before Mum gave birth to Michael, who would have been her first grandchild. I'd overheard Mum discussing this with Gran soon after my seventh birthday.

A dog walker had found Grandma Fay sprawled out on a stranger's doorstep, half-dead, almost frozen, and drenched in the pouring rain with her arm broken.

I glared at dad willing him to hurry with the visit. It was obvious he didn't want to be here either.

We stayed five minutes as Norman slept. Audrey had given him pills; he would sleep for hours.

Dad took hold of my hand, I let him, forgetting everything for a split second, but remembered what he'd done and pulled my hand away. "No, I don't want to hold your hand, you're the same as he is," I snapped pointing at his father on the settee. Dad didn't speak to me again.

A few days later, I had to go again.

"Why's it always me?" I demanded to know.

"Because Dad won't hurt you," answered Michael as I realised if he went, he would be at risk, that's why it had to be me.

"Okay, I'll go," I said, feeling guilty. It was true, Dad didn't hurt me as much as the others.

"Maybe you remind him of his sister when she was little, and that's why he doesn't beat you like us," said Michael.

46 NORMAN'S HOT BATH

We had to return several times to visit Norman. During one visit we arrived to find a huge tin bath in the middle of the dining room which was being utilized as a television room, bedroom, toilet, and bathroom, situated next to the kitchen. A bustle of activity was taking place.

I saw Audrey rush between rooms, filling the tin bath with boiling water she heated in alternate large pans on the gas ring in the small kitchen. She scurried in, carrying a huge pan with a long handle, as water splashed everywhere, the pan was too heavy and lopsided for her to carry safely. Audrey tipped the massive pan of water into the tin bath and all over the floor, noticing our presence, she said to Dad; "You need to lift your father and put him in the bath." She pointed to the settee where Norman lay, hidden under a thin towel, full of holes and yellow stains.

Together, Audrey and Dad lifted the old man's shivering, skeletal body and dropped him in the hot bath. He hadn't an ounce of flesh on him, his old bones must have felt the sudden impact of the metal beneath him. He screamed out, in agony.

I shouted; "You've dropped Norman!"

"It's too hot," Norman muttered. I heard him, no one else did. His old face looked livid and frantic; his eyes almost burst through their sockets. It was obvious he was in agony and terrified. Feeling revengeful, I hoped, he felt as frightened as he'd made Grandma Fay feel, on the day he'd robbed her and broken her arm.

Glaring at him, I tried to send him a telepathic message; "That's your punishment you bully, for hurting my grandma." Perhaps Dad and Audrey thought the same and dropped him in the scalding water as a form of revenge.

I stared at his old face, he looked identical to Dad, with thin lips, a long, thin drooping nose, cold narrow eyes, as blue as the sky. On anyone else, they would have been beautiful, but Norman was anything but, he was evil inside and out. It showed in his face, one that chilled me to the bone.

Was he the reason Dad and Aunt Jane were so horrid?

Audrey was beside herself and scurried back into the kitchen for cold water to pour over Norman, who was too weak to do anything other than sit and groan in agony, submerged in the scalding water as Dad tried to console him with words that didn't help.

"Why don't you take him out of the water?" I yelled, but no one answered me, so I went to sit on a chair, covered in smelly clutter and stared through the dirty window onto a dismal backyard.

I remembered Mum telling Gran how Grandma Fay had to go out looking for work every night, in all weathers, scrubbing steps for hours, then being beaten and robbed by her own husband, Norman.

Norman used to stand on the opposite side of the road, keeping watch, whilst Grandma Fay struggled in pain, on her bony, arthritic knees scrubbing step after step with cold water, then polishing the step with cardinal red wax polish, that stained her cold, hands red. Thinking about it made me feel sad for her. I wished she had met someone like Pop.

Dad and Audrey finished bathing Norman. They patted him dry, put clean pyjamas on him, ignoring his painful moans, then carried him to his makeshift bed, on the settee where they plonked him down, as he continued screaming out in pain.

Audrey rushed to get a ripped-up tea towel to bandage his arm, and anywhere else that displayed angry-looking scalded skin. I looked on in disgust. Her lack of hygiene was beyond disgraceful. Even I knew to use sterile bandages not grubby tea towels on wounds where the skin had peeled off.

I remembered how gentle and clean Gran and Pop had been with me when I scraped my knee after falling off my bike. They soothed my pain and rendered proper first aid, then explained how to look after wounds, with sterile dressings, and antiseptic cream. After which they gave me a caramel and a kiss on the cheek, which made me feel better.

Norman asked for Aunt Jane... "Where's my Jane? where's my Jane?"

"She had to go back to New York," Dad told him. "But Hattie's here," Dad added. Norman turned to look for me, his eyes twinkled at the mention of my name. His eyes searched for me, I ducked down, hoping he hadn't spotted me. "Please don't make me go to him, please!" I begged under my breath.

Norman's eyes closed for a second, his head dropped back, as Dad said, "Goodnight Dad."

Norman tried to sit up from his deathlike position. He shouted in a loud baritone voice, "Piss off Len, where's my Hattie? I want Hattie, I want Hattie!"

The power of his voice had grown stronger. Norman had been a baritone opera singer all his life, he seemed to have regained his vocal strength. I screamed and ran into the hallway; certain I'd seen a demon.

Dad followed me and shouted; "We'll come back, tomorrow Dad." Then we left.

We drove back to the house without a word. I kept thinking about how evil these people were and how sad it was to have them as relatives.

I wondered if Dad was trying to turn Mum into his downtrodden mother Fay, and Michael into himself and me into Aunt Jane, it seemed history was trying to repeat itself.

47 NORMAN DIES

The next morning, we returned to Norman's house to find him lying rigid on the settee, just as we'd left him the night before. The only difference was that his toothless mouth had dropped wide open. His eyes were closed. I thought he was dead.

The stench of urine hit us full-on as soon as we'd opened the front door, it smelled even worse when we entered the living room. Norman was drenched and soiled, lying in his own filth. Dad felt him and said he was freezing cold. I could see him shaking. His rough, dirty army blankets had dropped to the floor.

The thick drab curtains in his room were still drawn even though it was eleven in the morning. Dad opened them to let the daylight in. It seemed clear Audrey hadn't been in to check on him since we'd left the previous night.

I forced myself to look at him. He didn't have much longer in this world. I'd never get the chance to see him again after this visit.

Norman opened his eyes and stared. His pupils looked minute as his eyes darted from left to right. He seemed to strain for a moment, then came a stench of urine. He looked startled, then he passed, taking his abusive disgusting secrets with him. A few seconds later, I screamed as he made a guttural sound. Dad said it was the death rattle.

I looked at Dad; he was crying, I didn't know if it was from sadness or relief. My thoughts were only about Grandma Fay, Michael, Mum, and myself.

I heard a noise at the front door, Audrey came rushing in sounding breathless. "I'm back now, I nipped out for a minute, I've been here since seven... One of the children needed me." She was lying. I doubted if Dad noticed as he said nothing in response.

My theory was she'd disappeared the moment we left last night and hadn't returned. If she'd been here at seven, she wouldn't have left Norman in such a disgusting mess. I couldn't say anything as I had to remain seen and not heard. I knew, she'd left him to die in his filth, hoping we wouldn't notice, but I did, that was what I was good at. In fact, I excelled at observing the sneakiness of people and spotting lies and liars.

Mum said I had a sixth sense, clear vision, and a very old head on young shoulders. Michael said I was a nosy interfering busybody, a big-headed know it all, and a tell-tale! That made me laugh and seemed closer to the truth.

Audrey moved next to me and nudged me with her elbow. She whispered in my ear; "He's peed the bed."

"He died," I snapped back, wondering why she would tell me that, did she think it would make me giggle? She knew I didn't like him, but that didn't mean she could be disrespectful. Aunt Jane hadn't been paying Audrey to neglect and mock her father. She had been paid to look after him to the best of her ability. From the disgusting mess he'd been left to die in, she wasn't doing anything to the best of her ability at all.

I noticed another overpowering stench in the room, it made the urine fade into the background, bile rose in my throat, as I inhaled the smell of death.

I looked at Norman, the root cause of suffering and abuse of unimaginable degrees, he died, in front of my eight-year-old eyes. He was the man responsible for years of violence, neglect, and hatred which he'd passed to Dad and his sister, they took ownership of it, rather than resisting. Norman had left a legacy of hate.

I watched as Audrey closed Norman's eyelids to cover his staring cold eyes with her dirty fingers, then she placed germ-laden pennies on top to keep them shut.

48 TWISTED

Soon after Norman died, Dad journeyed back and forth to his childhood house to sort through mountains of clutter, which in turn became his. Fifty-plus years of rubbish soon filled up our overloaded house.

One evening, Dad returned from Norman's house to find Mum and me snuggling on the settee watching an episode of *Opportunity knocks* on television, we hadn't done this for a long time.

On opening the living room door, I saw that Dad looked furious. He stopped dead in his tracks, and looked down at us, with a face of hate. I heard him mutter something as he turned around and stormed upstairs. The banging that came from the bedroom above us was unnerving, it seemed he was furious. Minutes later I heard him enter the kitchen via the second door in the hallway, avoiding us.

The noises he made from the kitchen were louder than usual. We could hear the taps running at full force, and the violent clanking of dishes as he battled with the pots and pans. Next, he started singing profanities and made vicious threats against us, as he raged on.

There came a long pause in his singing, which alarmed us. The next thing we know, he's in the room, lifting me off the settee violently, by the scruff of my neck, then he flung me across the room to collide against the wall. I slithered to the floor, stunned. Turning to Mum, I saw she was still on the sofa, trying to get up to come to me, but Dad was too fast, he was on her, assaulting her rabidly, as I screamed hysterically, and pleaded for him to stop. Somehow, I was up again, tugging at his clothing, pushing, pulling, screaming, non-stop, he was oblivious. I saw he had hold of one of Mum's ankles, gripping it as tight as he possibly could with both hands, as Mum tried to lash out at him to no avail. Amidst the violent chaos, I saw as if in slow motion Dad begin twisting her leg round with all his might, incapacitating her, as her other leg lay trapped beneath her body. It seemed he wanted to twist it out of the socket, all Mum could do was yell, as I screamed alongside her.

Michael was out; Again, there was only me to help, I somehow moved away from the bedlam before me, and went behind Dad, to find myself grabbing at his shirt again, to pull him back as I had before. The difference now was I had grown inches taller and become stronger, but still a kid, against a grown angry man. I knew the drill and took hold, of his collar, tugging him. When I pulled, he twisted, Mum screamed. I tugged again, he twisted harder again, as Mum screamed louder.

No matter what I did, Mum's leg could very soon be wrenched out of the socket. It had become a battle of wills, and me being a young kid didn't know what to do, other than try what had worked once before, and act instinctively.

I hoped Dad wouldn't turn on me, so far, I had been let off lightly. He knew one hard punch to me would kill me, and then he'd be a murderer, so he put up with my hysterical efforts as I tried to save my loved one.

Dad had been trained as a fighter, he knew the holds, the limits, yet he went well beyond them. This time it seemed it wasn't just about him hating Mum, it was as if he was jealous of the love that we had, which we no longer had for him.

I let his shirt go, stepped away from his reach, as he concentrated on harming Mum. It was vital I did something more, so I jumped onto his back and dug my nails into his face, which startled him. My long fingernails ripped into his skin, as he yelled at me, and released his grip from Mum, I remained in place.

Mum tried to pull her leg away, but the monster had numbed it. I dug my nails deeper into his face as warm, sticky blood ran down my fingers.

"Let go you little bitch." He yelled as I did my best to dig in deeper. "Hattie, I'll fucking kill you" He hollered, so deeper in I dug. Dad stopped, perhaps my efforts had worked. He seemed to have had enough and slumped to the floor. After a moment, Dad got up clumsily. He didn't look at us as he scurried out of the room.

His usual bathroom routine began, bad noises, belching, chain pulling, taps running, and heavy footsteps on his way downstairs, then the slamming of the door, he'd gone out somewhere.

Mum tried to get up off the settee, but it was too painful for her to move; her leg was out of place, her face displayed her pain. "You need to go to the hospital Mum," I told her. "You need to call the Police." I knew she'd do neither, she was too scared to tell.

Then she quoted her marriage vows; "For better, for worse, for richer or poorer" as if repeating them would change our situation. We were living with the worse and poorer part of the vow. "Tell the police," I told her, still she refused. "If you don't I will,"

"You're a girl, they might not believe you. Hattie, it's a domestic problem, and I don't think they deal with domestics."

"What does that mean, a domestic?" I demanded to know.

"It means it happened in the house, so it's a civil matter," she gasped emotionally.

"So, if it happens in the street then it's bad, but in the house it's ok, it doesn't matter, is that right Mum?" I asked, my voice shaken. Mum didn't answer.

If only she'd called the police, Dad would be in the back of the police van going to prison, and Mum wouldn't have to go through any more violent attacks, nor would Michael, but she kept quiet and sobbed as did I. There had to be a reason for her silence.

49 LIFE GOES ON

The day of Norman's funeral arrived; Dad and Audrey attended, no one else. Dad wore his new tailor-made suit, courtesy of his sister, along with a new black tie and a mourning armband, displaying signs of respect for a man he loathed. We knew Dad hated Norman, we'd heard him sing songs about him, similar to those he sang about us. He said nothing on his return from the Wake, and life continued in the evil way that was now our norm.

Mum stayed off work on sick leave. She'd told the head of her department; she'd fallen off her bike and couldn't walk. It would take a long time for the dislocation to heal. She should have seen a doctor, and had her leg examined, and asked for a sick note, she'd receive no sick pay without that official note.

Dad had given her a warning. I heard him say; "Keep your bloody mouth shut or you'll regret it."

It took weeks for Mum's leg to feel near to normal again, she couldn't put her weight on it. The housework wasn't getting done.

We were at school all day. On our return, Mum told us we had to do the grocery shopping, and the cooking, we didn't know how to do either but soon learned.

Mum would write a list of what we needed to buy with the prices beside each item. She told us where to find the cheaper foods hidden at the rear of the bottom shelves and explained how to make a meal from our purchases.

We didn't see much of Dad during Mum's recovery, he stayed out most nights, only returning for clean clothes, which he'd had to wash and iron himself.

Michael suggested that Dad might be seeing another woman. Mum said she was welcome to him.

A month later, Mum felt she could go back to work. She felt safer there.

50 OPERA AND THE CINEMA

Dad played his opera records on repeat most Saturday mornings. His screeching arias became torturous as the house rattled with Madam Butterfly.

Michael and I decided not to hang around the house anymore. We left Dad to his ritual, making our escape through my bedroom window that had a veranda three feet below. It was barely wide enough for us to drop onto. From there we slid down the pole onto the path, then ran as fast as we could, away from the angry man and his forthcoming violence, that we knew he was psyching himself up for.

Michael often escaped through my bedroom window. He could leap right off the veranda roof and escape Dad's fury, as Dad played; catch and beat the kids. I would slip out through the front door and meet Michael a block away at our meeting place in times of desperation.

One-time Dad had found me cowering on the veranda roof, stuck, unable to move, I'd almost tumbled over the edge as I'd dropped from my window. I was scared of heights. Michael had already left the house as Dad was after him with a belt. I was too slow. Rather than help me back into my bedroom, Dad laughed, closed the window, and locked the latch. He left me there until Mum came home six hours later. I'd been stuck there in the pouring rain, crying my heart out. Michael didn't dare return to help me, as he knew Dad would drag him back into the house and beat the hell out of him.

This Saturday was different, we had a place to escape to.

On hearing the opera, having been turned to full blast, we scrambled through my window and dropped onto the ledge. Michael climbed down the pole first, then helped me, down the post. Once down, we ran away as fast as our legs would carry us, happy we were free.

We'd heard about a cinema a few miles away, showing Saturday morning matinees for children. We had a little pocket money to buy tickets and watch a film after which we'd walk back to the house.

It was our first time in a cinema, and we loved it, we'd found a new world, a happy one, if only for a few hours. We saw a film about a lost dog called Lassie, and became hooked, wanting to return to the cinema as soon as possible, to watch more.

On our return journey, to the house, we met other kids who immediately became our friends. An older boy with a cigarette in his mouth asked us if we were going to return the following week.

"I don't think we'll have enough money," said Michael. The boy laughed.

"Not a problem," he said. "What you need to do is bring an old birthday card, give it to the ticket seller at the kiosk and pretend it is your birthday. They'll let you in for free."

"It's not our birthdays," I chipped in.

"It doesn't matter, just say it is," laughed the boy. "The more kids on stage; the better it is for them."

The following weekend we arrived at the cinema; our old birthday cards stuffed in our pockets. I looked guilty and started shaking. Michael gave me a nudge as he often did to warn me to keep quiet and do nothing, apart from stay behind him. We got in with no questions asked. The cards were our free passes.

We sat in the comfy, burgundy, velvet seats, delighted by our trickery, and reclined happily, to watch the adverts and wave to kids from school dotted around the audience.

The adverts stopped midway. Heavy curtains that matched our seats were drawn, across the screen.

A man appeared on stage holding a microphone, wearing a striped suit and red bow tie, calling out names with great enthusiasm. To our shock, we heard him announce; "Today we have a brother and sister sharing a birthday. Hattie and Michael Thompson, please come on up to the stage." We stood up in shock and started moving towards the man.

"Let's have a huge round of applause for Hattie and Michael Thompson."

The entire audience clapped, cheered, and stamped their feet wildly, which stunned both of us. We looked to the boy who'd told us the scam, he was laughing hysterically, giving us the thumbs up.

"Come on kids, I can't hear you!" Shouted the compere into the microphone to encourage more noise. "Let's have a serious, exceptionally loud round of applause for these two children, and wish them a very happy birthday. Hattie Thompson is five today and Michael, her big brother is seven. Many happy returns of the day!"

The kids cheered, popcorn flew like confetti, as we passed through rows of excited kids, slapping us on our backs, congratulating us.

We'd never felt so embarrassed.

I didn't look five, nor Michael seven, we were taller than most of the other kids of our ages, we looked like teenagers.

The next thing that happened, was an organist rose from under the stage on a noisy platform, playing the birthday tune repeatedly. All the excited kids continued in their frenzy as others came up onto the stage to join us.

We focused on the organist's shiny bald head lit up by the spotlights, as the rising platform came to a juddering halt.

Remaining in line with thirty other kids, we guessed a few had genuine birthdays, the rest, were the same as us, with fake ones. I'd never felt so guilty.

When the organist's platform drew almost level with the stage, the compere instructed us to face forward and shout into the microphone; "Thank you very much," to the young, over-excited audience. We were told to march in time to the music as the organist resumed playing until the charade ended, and someone handed us free tickets for the matinee the following week.

After the pomp and ceremony, before we left the stage, we posed for photographs, then returned to our seats.

We hadn't laughed so much in ages. Michael and I deserved this birthday celebration to make up for the ones we'd never had.

The following week we saw our photograph in the local paper and hoped Dad wouldn't see it. He'd soon put a stop to our fun if he had.

At last, we had a happy safe place to escape to, out of Dad's way.

51 ABDUCTION

A while after yet more attacks in our house, I was playing alone in the ginnel between our house and the neighbours; Mr. and Mrs. Burney, who had three sons; a lot older than us who we rarely saw. Next door to them lived Mark Willis.

Mr. Burney was a foul-mouthed man, we could hear him on Saturday nights, coming home drunk, returning from the local pub, shouting and swearing as he trundled down the street. Sometimes I could hear him throwing up in the gutter by our shared middle gate.

Through my bedroom window, I could see and hear everything and would peep out to investigate the slightest sound. Being a light sleeper, I often looked through my window late at night. Being a curious child, I needed to know what was happening.

Mr. Burney was another neighbour Mum told us to keep away from at all costs. She had a terrible feeling about him. Our lives were bad enough, the last things we needed were more problems.

I was off school this day, recovering from dental surgery. The dentist had removed four teeth a few days previously. He'd told me I had too many teeth, then yanked four out. Michael told me before I left the house, that dentists used laughing gas to stop the pain, but I hurt, and I wasn't laughing. I hadn't wanted the gas, and I'd fought in my chair, to keep the gas mask away from my face, to no avail. An hour later, after my ordeal, I'd walked back to our house, with four teeth attached to large bloodied roots wrapped in tissue as a memento.

I'd been so dizzy-making my way back home alone. I seemed to have taken six steps forward and twelve steps backwards, but somehow, I made it to the house.

Once in, I collapsed on the settee and puked all over the floor. Mum found me later in a wretched mess, she said I was to stay off school until I felt better. There was no one to stay home with me as she and Dad both worked.

By the third day, I felt a lot better and decided to get a little fresh air, so I went to play in the ginnel, on what was a dull wet day. I'd been playing for about five minutes when Mr. Burney appeared at the top of the ginnel and asked me if I was all right. He'd heard me playing two a ball against the brick wall on our side of the house.

"I'm fine," I informed him. He smiled at me, displaying yellow teeth with several gaps, then returned to whence he came. Just a few minutes later he was back again; "Is everything still all right Hattie?" He asked, this time from the bottom of the ginnel, close to the walls and gardens, which were overgrown with hedges and tall hollyhocks, making it dark there. He looked concerned, which made me feel something was wrong. I wondered why he was asking again, I'd told him already, I was fine.

Mr. Burney had the droopiest jowls and eyelids I'd ever seen on anyone; the whites of his eyes were pink and yellow. Mum said she thought he had yellow Jaundice from a bad liver. According to local gossip, he was always in the off-license buying whiskey and beer. At night he was in the pub guzzling even more booze, hence the jaundiced look and the huge beer belly overlapping his thighs. His face was bloated, his nose covered with purple veins and open pores.

Every time I saw him, his shirt buttons were open, displaying a rug of long grey chest hair, at the top, and his belly button below. I was certain he dressed like that to shock us, which he did.

I remembered Mum's warnings; "Don't go near him, there's something strange about him, that gives me the creeps." It was another gut instinct she had. Mum reiterated the same warning many times, to make her point clear.

Mr. Burney called me over to him, I couldn't hear what he was saying. I expected his wife would be nearby, she was usually hovering around with her curlers in and her apron on. Mrs. Burney hardly ever spoke, she seemed too nervous to even say, "hello."

I assumed he wanted to ask me something, so I moved a little closer, but not too close, remembering Mum's warnings. He mumbled incoherently, pointing to his throat, showing he had some kind of problem with his voice. "I'm Sorry Mr. Burney I can't hear you," I told him, moving a little closer, towards the closed gate, thinking I would be all right. He wasn't coming into the ginnel, otherwise, he would have opened his gate. "Are your parents' home Hattie?"

"No Mr. Burney, they're at work," I replied.

"What time will they be back?" He asked with urgency and excitement.

"I don't know, maybe in an hour or two, I'm not sure," I told him.

"Where's Michael, is he around?" He asked, edging closer. I thought he was having an attack of bronchitis because his breathing sounded like Dad's.

"He's at school. Should I tell my parents you want something when they come home?" I asked, wondering where all this questioning was leading. I wanted to get away as soon as I could.

"Sorry, I can't hear you, Hattie, come a little closer," he motioned with his hand, touching his ear to settle the fact he was a little hard of hearing.

Out of politeness, I moved a fraction of an inch closer, and that's when he grabbed me. Mr. Burney pounced on me so fast, that I couldn't dodge him. He tugged and pulled at me, dragging me up and over the closed gate as if I were a sack of potatoes, after which he ran through the open back door into his dirty kitchen that stank of sprouts and vinegar, with me tucked under his sweaty armpit.

I tried my hardest to escape, kicking out at him frantically, yet only meeting the air. He had me in a lock I couldn't escape, I was going nowhere, other than where he wanted to put me. It was impossible for me to scream for help as his hand gagged me. He moved fast and with such strength, crushing me under his strong arm. His putrid stench and hold were suffocating me.

"Keep still you little bitch. Don't you bloody move," he threatened in a terrifying voice. His breathing was heavy and rapid. He stank of stale cigarettes and beer and a total lack of hygiene. Michael and I often criticized his disgusting shirts with massive sweat stains under his arms, and his rotten teeth and brown gums, they were like Mr. Davis's, the substitute teachers.

He pressed his rough, dirt-engrained, calloused hand against my mouth. I could taste something vile through his split skin. His other hand gripped me, as he carried me off. I didn't think I would get out of this.

The skin on his rough hands scratched the skin on my delicate face. His grip was cutting off my blood source as I struggled and fought with a vengeance. Desperately I fought to thrash my way out of his vice-like grip to get away from him.

I couldn't breathe through my nose, I'd never been able to, I had to depend on my mouth and Mr. Burney was suffocating me to a point where I almost passed out, not only with fear but also with asphyxiation. My entire body trembled, spasm after horrific spasm, engulfed with fear, I knew I was a lamb to the slaughter.

Mr. Burney bundled me into his living room, as I fought to save my own life, and make my escape, using everything I had. It was impossible, he was on his mission. I couldn't wriggle out of this, nor could I scream.

This old man was so violent with me I needed to vomit, but it wouldn't come up. Mr. Burney didn't care how hurt or how terrified I was, he would not let me go. I could tell he was happy and that his adrenaline was pumping away as Dads did. This horrid man had abducted me, crossed the line, there was no going back for him, nor for me, this was more abuse I would have to live with and never forget, that is if I got out alive. "Please help me someone please help me," I begged, but I knew from experience begging doesn't help, no one listens, no one cares, there was only me that could help myself.

This had been planned, he'd struck when he had the opportunity he needed, the man was a coward. Mr. Burney knew I was alone, he'd been watching and waiting, checking everyone's whereabouts, and timescales, to ensure he was clear to snatch me, just like Mark Willis had.

Mr. Burney secured me in his criminal grip, one heavy leg moved over the top of me to weigh my legs down. One arm was free to abuse me, his other hand, clamped over my mouth.

His almost bald, bulbous head went backwards for a second, his hand slackened from across my mouth. As soon as my mouth was uncovered, I managed to scream, then his sloppy face was on mine, shoving his disgusting fat tongue into my mouth, immediately choking me. I gagged from revulsion as bile rose to the back of my throat.

He recoiled for a moment, and I clamped my mouth shut, but it was a struggle as I kept gagging. Using his free hand, he pulled at my cheeks, babbling on with words I could not understand, as he leered at me with glazed eyes.

His huge, floppy body flattened me further down on his settee, winding and imprisoning me. I opened my mouth to gasp for breath, and his tongue shot back in.

I kept trying to shake my head and say NO! and push against him, to get him off me, thrashing to escape, but my movements were restricted by his huge form. I was going nowhere.

At this time, I was almost ten years old; he was older than Dad and he knew I hated what he was doing. He knew I didn't want him shoving his putrid tongue in my mouth and he knew I was terrified, but he didn't care. He was intent on doing exactly what he wanted to do, ignoring my anguish, and the very fact that what he was doing was criminal.

All I had to fight back with were my teeth. My mouth and gums were still sore after the dental work, but they were all I had, to save myself with.

The minute I caught my breath, his big head with piggy eyes, came back at me, his tongue re-emerged. I bit down as hard as I could, trying to bite through its tip. My teeth clamped down with all the strength I could muster and thankfully my timing was spot on. My breathing was getting worse as I struggled to fight for my life.

I ground down hard. It was all knocking me sick, the terror, the stench and taste of his rancid tongue mixed in with the decaying teeth and the disgusting stench of his body odour and his dirty house.

I was hurting him but it wasn't enough, it was temporary, he would not let me go. This old man was enjoying my struggle and my fight back, just as Dad did. I was a prize he'd had his eye on for some time, even though I was young, the same age as his granddaughter Julie.

My hands became free, enabling me to grab at his floppy jowls, cow biting his blood-red face, which bore the same strange expression as Dad's face which knocked me even sicker as I knew now what Dad wanted. Their faces continued alternating, in my mind, as if they were the same man.

It seemed unlikely I'd make it out of here. I'd have to die fighting him off, I wanted it to stop, it was so wrong in a multitude of ways, there was nothing right, about any of this. His mission was well underway. His goal was to violate my innocence.

He cared nothing about the fact that he was destroying a life, my life, the sad one I was trying to preserve in the house next door.

Miraculously, I projectile vomited hot bile, his putrid tongue recoiled quicker than it had gone in. My vomit saved me as it pumped out like a hot geyser, through my mouth, and nose, it wouldn't stop.

There was a bang, a door slamming, it came from the kitchen, probably it was his wife, he panicked, as I continued heaving acidic bile, over his dirty settee and over him.

Pushing him out of my way, I escaped and found myself screaming hysterically and gasping for air. It was difficult to run, as my shaky legs struggled to carry me, and I didn't know where to go.

I found myself in the outhouse by our back door, next to the coal shed, huddled in the corner where I rocked back and forth, sat as far behind the toilet basin as I could get, trying to comfort myself. I was terrified Mr. Burney would come after me to finish what he'd started. I'd locked the door as soon as I entered this disgusting, cold room. All I could do was sit, rock, and stare at the door.

Mum and Dad returned to the house from work hours later. I heard shouting, it would be Dad bullying Mum again It was impossible for me to help her this time, I wasn't able to move, I was a child. It was me that needed help.

I heard Mum in the garden, calling my name, she sounded frantic. She couldn't find me and I was too shocked to call out. I wanted to sit in place until I died, this world was disgusting, I hated it so much.

It had grown dark, and I didn't dare move to switch the light on. I heard Michael calling for me, pleading for me to go to him. I wanted to call out to him, but couldn't, I was scared of making any sound, or moving an inch.

Even Dad shouted my name. No way in this world would he be the one I went to; he was as bad as Mr. Burney.

Nobody thought to search the outhouse straight away, I'd heard them run past. It was the last place they looked; Michael was the one who tried to open the door. He'd heard me, as I fought to hold back my sobs. He and Mum tried the handle, it wouldn't open, they banged until they forced it open. They found me shaking, my knees up to my chin, almost hypothermic and terrified.

Their faces when they saw me were chilling. "What happened Hattie?" Mum asked softly, as she put the light on and bent over me, holding her arms out for me to go into. I could only push myself back against the wall.

"Hattie, it's Mum, come to me, sweetheart. Let me get you out of here. Come on, come." I flew into her arms and clung to her, as she helped me out of the squalid outhouse, taking me back into the house I hated.

"Mr. Burney," I managed to mutter through my swollen lips that tasted of blood and vomit. My dress was soaking wet and covered in cold sick, clinging to my legs, the way it felt made me heave.

"Tell me, Hattie, what did he do to you?" Asked Mum, her face concerned, I was so used to seeing her face like this.

I spluttered; "He... he dragged me into his house and he, he put his t... t... tongue in my mouth." Dad disappeared within seconds on hearing this. Mum followed at his heel as Michael sat with me holding my hand.

Seconds later, there was banging, it was Mum or Dad hammering the front door knocker next door, shouting threats and swear words, "Come on out you slimy bastard, get out of your fucking house, come on you bloody coward, and get what you deserve!" it was Dad's voice, then more voices yelling. Then a new voice shouted; "What's all the bloody noise?"

Michael and I sat and waited as the banging and crashing outside continued. It was the only time in my life that I hoped Dad had lost his temper, worse than he'd ever done in our house.

Mum returned to my side, upset. I never got to know what happened; all she said was never to go near him or his family ever again, they were disgusting, and that she and Dad had sorted it out.

The Burney family did a moonlight flit two nights later. One minute they were there, the next the house was empty. That's what a lot of neighbours did. They flit in the middle of the night, hoping no one would see them go. We often saw large vans or several cars parked outside various houses, being loaded up with shabby furniture, as neighbours did a runner. Some for not paying the rent, others wanted by the police. There were many reasons that caused them to vanish into the night. Everyone saw them leave but said nothing.

52 FRIDAY THE THIRTEENTH

Bad things always happened to us, one horrific event after the other, yet we battled on, hoping one-day things would get better.

To this day, I don't know how we got through any of it, many wouldn't have survived. Mum said we were strong mentally and physically and that we needed to remain strong and look to the future as things could only get better.

It was Friday the thirteenth. The kids in my class said it was an unlucky, cursed day, but for us, every day seemed cursed.

I'd walked partway home from school with a new friend, then made my way to the house, took out my key, and attempted to open the door. The key wouldn't go into the keyhole. I tried several times, then gave up, and waited for Mum or Michael to return.

Mum arrived on her bike at the same time as Michael, I'd been sitting on the doorstep for over an hour. Mum had been at work, Michael at school, it took him an hour and a half to get home on two buses, as his new school was miles away across the city.

"What's wrong," Mum asked.

"I can't get in; the key won't turn," I stressed as the neighbours from next door came rushing out. Stevie snatched the key from my hand and tried to open our front door to no avail. We checked around the outside of the house, looking for open windows, so Michael could climb in, all were locked.

"It's strange Mrs. Thompson," said Stevie, smirking. His voice sounded odd, too polite; he was trying to come across as innocent by taking it up an octave. I hoped his goody two shoe's act had alerted Mum as it had me. The kids at school used that tone when they'd been caught doing something bad. I watched as he and his suspicious-looking brothers followed us around the outside of the house, sniggering as if they'd been bad, though, at that time, I had no idea what they had really done.

"We need to break a window," Mum said. Michael broke a tiny kitchen window, put his hand through the jagged gap to unlatch the larger one. Mum gave him a leg up, then he clambered through, taking a head dive, just missing the sink full of soaking pots and pans, I'd been watching and felt guilty as I giggled nervously. Once upon his feet, Michael opened the back door, and we piled into the house, neighbours included.

As soon as we entered, we felt the chill of fear; as if the house was haunted.

"Check the front door," Mum told Michael.

Michael returned looking troubled... "The front door's been locked from the inside," he said.

"How is that possible?" Mum asked, perplexed. I saw the brothers from next door nudge each other. As a group, we ventured from room to room. The neighbours whispered as they lagged behind us, not taking any of this seriously.

Turning towards them I said... "Thanks for your help, you can go now," Mum added her thanks, and they left.

"We've been burgled!" Michael shouted from upstairs. Mum ran to join him. I heard her sad, voice; "Oh no, oh no, what a mess, how dreadful, how dreadful, everything's ruined."

I forced myself upstairs on legs that had become weak with fear, to see what had happened.

Vandals had been in; they'd destroyed as much as they could. Each bed had been defecated or urinated on. The pillows were soaked, others had been emptied of their feathers and spread across the room as if whoever had been in had a pillow fight.

Smeared human excrement marked the bedroom walls. All the drawer's contents had been tipped onto the floor, then doused in liquid chemicals. Dad's luxurious aftershave had been sprayed ad-lib until empty. "They don't want us to have anything," I mumbled.

It had taken Mum a long time to earn the money to buy what we had. She'd worked hard, cycling to work in all weathers, five miles there, five miles back, on her homemade bike. Dad hadn't contributed a penny to what we had; he'd saved his money somewhere. Maybe the burglars knew he had a stash of hidden money and were looking for it.

Everything we owned, regardless of how cheap or old it was, mattered to us. We respected what we had and how it had been earned. The vandals had decided Mum's hard work meant nothing; our destroyed possessions were their cheap laugh.

We couldn't tell if anything was missing, it dawned on me nothing would have been taken as I remembered Katie's nasty words, which she'd spat out at me years ago... "You're poor, ya've nothing like this little lot Hattie Thompson!"

Her mean words came back to haunt me, and how she'd rubbed my nose in the fact we had nothing of value. She'd been right, to others our possessions were worth nothing monetary-wise, but to us, they were everything, because it was all we had.

The police came, they checked everywhere, looking for the point of entry and evidence. Eventually, after hours of detective work, they discovered the burglars had entered through the roof, that's where the strange noises had been coming from.

From that day on I was even more terrified, it became a ritual of mine to check behind doors, under beds, inside cupboards, constantly looking for burglars. I'd lie awake, listening for noises, unable to sleep, concentrate or relax; everything and everyone had become so evil and there was nothing I could do to change any of it. The only option I had was to survive, and look forward, as Mum said we should do.

We still had the worry of Dad's violent assaults and Sally James was still bugging me daily, the teachers weren't the calmest either and had been dishing out all sorts of physical punishments. Nowhere was safe.

53 POP DIES

A few months after the burglary, Pop had a second heart attack. The doctor told Gran he should stay at home; it would distress him if he were to be taken to hospital. His final days should be with those he loved in familiar surroundings.

Mum cycled to their house daily, her siblings had been only once. They said their cold, heartless goodbyes and left as quickly as they'd arrived, offering no help or support to Gran.

Pop had been sleeping in the living room; Mum had positioned his bed next to the pretty bay window, so he could look out and see his beautiful garden. He'd watch his neighbours pass by, who waved to him and smiled. The men tipped their hats out of respect to Pop.

Mum stayed the night with Gran, together, they sat by Pop's side. The doctor stayed too, sat on a chair in the corner of the room.

At dawn, Mum returned to check on Michael and me, concerned we were alone with Dad. The minute she entered the house, the phone rang... It was the doctor calling from our Grandparents' house. "Pop's at peace now," Mum told us, having just lost her hero, the man who'd taught her so much, the man who adored his family, who sang, laughed, and made items to please us all. He brought joy and love to everyone, especially to us... Our loss was enormous.

We hugged and cried in grief. Dad ignored the distraught scene and buried himself in his newspaper.

Mum was devastated, she asked Dad to take her back to Gran's house in the car, as she was too shaky to ride her bike. Dad refused. Mum set off, in the in-climate weather to cycle back to the house of loss, alone, regardless of how she felt, she needed to be with Gran.

A week later, the rest of the family arrived to attend the funeral, there was a large gathering of friends, neighbours, colleagues, and acquaintances, the church was packed with those who wanted to say their goodbyes, and others who wanted a free meal at the end of the service.

Later, during the Wake Uncle Barry sneaked out to Gran's house, leaving the rest of us at the local hotel where refreshments were served, whilst family members bickered over who was entitled to what! I spotted him skulk out, trying to be discreet.

On our return to Gran's house, we found what Uncle Barry had done after he'd sneaked off. He'd destroyed the wonderful creations Pop had made, without asking Gran. All the woodwork he had spent hours building into furniture had been smashed into pieces and left in a pile. The fountain had also been demolished.

Mum shouted at him; "You're an inconsiderate fool. How dare you? "Uncle Barry couldn't have done anything worse. Gran was devastated and demanded to know why he'd been so thoughtless. He said he thought they'd be too distressing for her to look at.

"Do you think I wouldn't want to be reminded of the man I loved with all my heart?" she sobbed. "Pop made everything out of love, and you didn't have the decency to ask or the respect to wait."

Uncle Barry drove off in a fury, leaving Gran heartbroken and in tears. That was the last time Gran saw him.

I'd been sitting on the stairs, with Michael, both of us listening and watching. I thought of him and Aunt Jane and how insensitive he was.

He'd seemed impressive when I first saw him step out of his car. That changed when I saw him slobbering over Aunt Jane, it was then that I saw him as a pompous fool who thought a cigar and a baritone voice made him important.

Later, Michael and I sat in a corner of the room, to eavesdrop on a discussion about Gran and her house. One said the house would be too big for Gran now she was alone, and she should live in a care home. Another said the house should be sold, and the money divided. Gran heard every word.

We felt sorry for Gran, as Aunt Sarah, Uncle Barry, and Uncle Keith, saw her as a burden and a meal ticket. No one, other than Mum, Michael, and I wanted her, the others wanted her house, money, and anything else they could get their greedy hands on. Unbeknownst to them, Aunt Sarah had already taken the antiques and anything else of value during her rare visits. She'd beaten everyone to it.

Mum said Gran could stay with us, but first, she'd have to clear it with Dad. Gran needed looking after. Michael and I felt concerned about her staying in our house, it wasn't safe there. Dad was the last man on earth that should be near her, this would put her at risk. To our surprise, Dad agreed. Gran could stay, but she'd have to pay for the privilege. His demands for money caused a huge argument as Mum pointed out how Gran and Pop had helped him in years gone by, lending him money, and giving him support emotionally. Gran should live with us free Mum stressed, but Dad wouldn't listen, he wanted payments and payments he would have.

Gran's stay lasted three days. I walked into the living room and found Dad bent over her, leering into her face, insulting and physically threatening her… "I hope you have a Heart attack and die, you're an old cow. I'll give you a bloody good hiding, I don't care how bloody old you are," he yelled. I heard Gran beg; "Go away, leave me alone, please Len, leave me alone!" It looked like Dad was about to hit her, so I charged at him, as fast as I could to knock him out of the way. Gran's freshly brewed tea was on the table by her side, I grabbed it and splashed it in Dad's face just as he tried to retaliate. He wiped the hot tea from his face and shouted; "I expect the old bag gone when I get back," then stormed out.

Dad could easily have turned on me, but something always held him back from beating me, I had no idea what it was, but somehow, I knew my days were numbered.

Mum arrived soon after, to find Gran shaking uncontrollably as I cradled her in my arms, desperate to console her. "We'll get you home Mum. Hattie, pack Gran's things. I'll call a taxi." Mum tapped out the telephone number for a cab, as the lock was still on. We took her home, and I promised to stay with her as often as I could.

That week I stayed off school. Mum didn't know I was with Gran during the days. I'd written my own sick note to the school, as my place was with Gran, not the class. Gran was in need, in mourning, and in shock. Thanks to Pop I had excellent handwriting, I could write like Mum and Dad, in fact, anyone, Pop had taught me to write in many styles. I could do them all, better than everyone. I was a handwriting artist, a copycat, that was my prodigy. Once I'd completed my sick note, replicating Mum's elaborate script, I said, "Thanks Pop," as if he were watching me. I wrote;

Dear Mr. Morrison,

Hattie is not well enough to attend school for the foreseeable future due to gastric enteritis, if she is no better after five days, I will take her to see the doctor, but for now, she needs bed rest and quiet.

Yours sincerely, H. Thompson. (Mrs.)

It was fortunate we had a medical dictionary to hand. Michael knew what I was doing and suggested tummy upsets as no one wanted to talk about those. We flicked through the book of illnesses, diseases, and gory photographs, educating ourselves for the current excuse and others for the future. We used the medical terminologies for maximum effect. With my skill, I could take more days off without question should Gran ever need me.

Gran wasn't pleased with my forging letters, she'd always been strict where school attendance was concerned, but she laughed when I told her, and promised not to tell. She needed me and I needed her. For the entire week I took her mind off the vile abuse she'd suffered from Dad and helped her grieve over Pop. We enjoyed each other's company so much. She told me tales about herself growing up, and how Pop had wooed her. Gran was an absolute comic, and a joy to be with. She cried often for Pop, she missed him so much. We cuddled and cried together. I missed him too.

Mum and Michael kept a check on us, arriving on their bikes early in the evening and leaving at ten pm, so we could go to bed, as Mum thought I needed to be up early for school, she didn't know about my truancies.

54 MARK'S COMEUPPANCES

Once Gran felt stronger, I returned to school. I later called back at Dad's house to collect various items I needed. On my arrival, I noticed Mark Willis playing ball in front of our hedge bouncing a tennis ball with one hand, the other hand perched on his hip, staring at me as I walked towards the gate.

Not wanting a confrontation, I ignored him and went into the house. Mum told me later that Dad was away, so I stayed overnight.

The next morning, I was up early and went to the front door to bring in the bottles of milk off the doorstep. As I opened the door, I spotted Mark ducking and diving behind our hedge. Realising I'd spotted him, he put his fist up threateningly, and called me a 'crybaby.' I guessed he'd seen me crying when we set off to the funeral, we were dressed in black, and I'd been distraught as Mum held my hand and led me to the car.

He ran to the top of our path, just as I was about to take the milk bottles into the house. "Are you ready for another beating Hattie Thompson? Aww did someone die?"

Then he said nasty things about funerals, death, and Pop, whom he'd never met, doing his best to upset me. Mark achieved his goal quickly; I walked up to him and told him to leave me alone and not be horrible.

He raised his arm to hit me, that was his mistake. I'd been waiting for this; I'd known it was coming. Instinctively I grabbed his arm and pulled him downwards. Mark looked confused; his confidence had disintegrated. Did he think I would stand there and do nothing? It seemed he hadn't expected that move, it was another one Dad had taught us and one Michael let me practice with him until it became second nature.

Mark swore and tried to spit at me, but his head was down, so the spit landed on his shoe as threats spewed out of his mouth. He wanted to beat me up, worse than he had on that dreadful path when I was seven years old.

"You bitch, I'll beat the shit out of you, this time, I'll really beat you!" he screamed at me. "Like you did on the path? You're a sneaky coward, a mard, cowardly shit. I don't think you'll do that to me ever again, not after today!" I told him.

Without notice, I released his arm and latched on to his ears with both hands, and positioned his head at knee level, just where I wanted him. I brought my knee up to his face, then pummelled him fifty times to the dozen as he screamed out, hysterically. As one leg tired, I switched to the other, until I was spent and he was sobbing in a bloodied heap on the floor."

"See Mark, I was ready for you, more than bloody ready, are you ready to go again? perhaps one more round? You cry-baby, aww did the small girl beat you up?" I asked him feeling calm and quite triumphant.

Remembering the snow and grit, he shoved in my mouth, I scooped up a handful of soil from the flower bed next to Mark, and said;

"You made me eat grit and snow, now Mark Willis, eat this." He shook his head, becoming frantic, as I rubbed the muck against his mouth, and over his face, just as he'd done to me. I had his hair secured tight in my other hand, rendering him powerless. I let the muck drop to the floor after a few hard rubs...

"Just toying with you Mark, I won't make you eat it as you did me!" I told him. Then gave him my best advice, the same as Dad had often given us, yet gone against;

"Mark, repeat after me eight times... Boys don't hit girls." He did as he was told. Next, I gave him his final warning...

"If you ever start on me again, I'll finish it and I may not be as nice next time, and I will call the police." By this time Mark was sobbing hysterically; "Who's the little cry baby now Mark?" I asked.

"I am," he spluttered. Giving him a few slaps across both cheeks, as he'd done to me, I gave him a really hard one as a finale, and let him go, watching him as he ran away, headed home, yelling. Again, I'd protected myself, from what could have been an even nastier attack, I'd prevented any future harassment and bullied the bully, giving him, a taste of his own medicine and he hadn't liked it.

Later, when Mum returned to the house from work, Mark's mother rushed to our house banging the door knocker and ringing the bell frantically. Mum answered the door. "What's all the noise?" Mum asked. Mrs. Willis shouted at her;

"I'll tell you what all the bleeding noise is, look what your bloody Hattie's done to our Mark." Mark stood at the top of our path, biting his nails, sobbing his heart out, as I stood behind Mum, mouthing to him 'cry-baby,' showing him my fist, just as he had done to me. His plan had backfired.

"If Hattie did something to him, then I can assure you he deserved it, have you forgotten how he beat her up on the path on her way home from school? The sneaky so and so, you need to sort your son out, he's dangerous. He's been loitering around our hedge for ages, waiting to attack my daughter. We've all been watching him, sadly we weren't around to help her this morning, otherwise, we'd have dragged him to the Police Station. Look at the size of him, he's a head taller than Hattie. Not only that, he's three years older. You need to get him some serious help. Now get off my path, keep your son away from my children, or I will call the police and the social services, then we'll see what they have to say!" Mrs. Willis scurried off, dragging Mark by the ear. I laughed as she walloped him across his ear once she thought they were out of sight. Mark never spied, threatened, or stalked me again after that day.

Gran was trying to keep busy and was feeling a lot better, especially now Mum, Michael and I took turns keeping her company. Dad stayed away from the house a lot; he was elsewhere being entertained in ways we as children didn't want to think about. I was back at school, trying my best to separate school life, from home life. It was vital for me to concentrate on my school work, and learn as much as I could so I could pass my exams, as I had a future to plan for. I'd be going to a High school after the summer, I needed good grades.

55 NEW FAMILY

It was the summer of 1970, Aunt Jane had been on another yearly visit, during which she and Dad had disappeared for the duration of her stay. We had no idea where they went and no interest.

Another new family moved down our road, they turned up out of the blue. I was so happy, as they had ten children, two around my age. I'd hoped to make friends with them, which I did, immediately.

The whole family liked me and practically took me in as one of their own. I spent hours at their house even though they were always busy, yet they made time for me and fed me if I was still there at mealtimes. Thiers was quite a happy home, where they worked with each other, rather than against each other, unlike Dad. I remember they always had the kettle on the stove and always stew and dumplings, and if they had something, they shared it, which was quite a rarity down our road.

My new friend Maggie told me she liked ice skating and swimming, she wanted me to go with her, but I didn't have enough money. I still took my rightful pocket money out of Dad's pocket, but it wasn't enough, as I was saving up for emergencies.

"Hattie, I'll tell you an easy way to get money," she said. "You need to collect beer bottles, pop bottles, and soda siphons. Once you have a few, return them to the off-license, and they'll buy them off you for a few pennies for each bottle. The siphons will get you maybe two shillings.

I loved that idea. She and I scouted the neighbourhood, every chance we got, filling our mother's shopping bags and potato sacks, with so many glass bottles we could hardly carry them all. We found most of them dumped under bushes around the estate, then hauled them to the off-license, cashed them in, and split the money.

On the first Saturday of each month, we would watch a matinee, we didn't use the birthday card trick anymore, as we could pay to go in now with our bottle money. I would spend every second Saturday at the local swimming baths, where Maggie taught me how to somersault dive. We were let in without charge sometimes, as a lifeguard wanted to date her. Sundays we'd ice skate for hours.

When it was almost closing time at the rink, we'd collect the empty bottles people had left under the seats and return them to the cafe. We always had enough money from that, to fund our next outing. It seemed no one knew about the bottle payments, so they were ours. Thanks to Maggie, I had some happy times that kept me sane.

56 SCHOOL FIGHT

Things were going well for me at last. I had my weekends to look forward to with my friend Maggie. I stayed with Gran overnight, three or four times a week. Dad was busy freelancing on weekends taking wedding photographs. Sometimes we wouldn't see him for days.

My peace ended at school on a Friday, I knew it wouldn't last. Sally's day of sorting me out once and for all had finally arrived, this was her last chance, as we'd be leaving this school soon, to move on to our respective High schools, she was going to a local school, I was going to another school miles away.

Sally had waited so long for this day, her jealousy had been festering, in preparation to destroy me, before we moved on with our lives. It surprised me that it had taken her almost four years to make her move.

Over time, I'd become accustomed to her constant spying on me from the shadows, and her efforts to intimidate me to get me to react, but I didn't respond, and that upset her even more. I too was ready for this nonsense to come to an end, it was time for closure, time for her to leave me alone. I wanted my life to be normal, one where I didn't need to look over my shoulder every day, I had enough of that in the house with Dad.

My instincts told me this was the day Sally James would try to make me suffer, as she seemed more psyched up than usual and had been goading me ever since I entered the school grounds.

During the morning break, Sally and her gang stood outside the washroom entrance, laughing at what I wore as I entered. Sally didn't seem aware that her own clothes were as bad as mine. She stared at the bruises on my arms, remnants of recent attacks at the house where I'd got bumped as I pushed my way in between Mum and Dad, trying to help her. Michael was bruised too, but he managed to give Dad a black eye during the last battle. I guessed Sally thought anyone with bruises like mine must be a hard case, a challenge for her to defeat. If she beat me, she'd reign supreme as the one who battered Hattie Thompson, the bruised girl. It would be her claim to fame, her Legacy. She'd go down in the playground's history as the `Cock of the girls, ´ and to her, that would be some kind of achievement, which I found very sad.

I wondered what she would think if she knew how I came by my injuries. I doubted she would feel sorry for me even if she knew the truth.

Somehow, I knew her obsession with me hadn't been about the French horn at all, that had been her excuse. I decided she had two reasons for picking on me, the first was she didn't like me, yet she didn't know me. The second was she didn't like herself and thought taking out her insecurities on me would make her feel better. I may have been wrong, but whatever her problem was, I would not let her take them out on me, nor was I going to cower. I'd face her and get it over with.

Whatever happens, this day would soon be behind me, then perhaps she would leave me alone, and we could both move on.

We sat in class. The morning break had almost finished. I could hear a lot of whispering and planning going on but had no idea what the kids in my class were so excited about as no one said anything to me, not until Ricky Doyle plonked himself on top of my desk, and shoved a note in my face. I took it out of his hand and read it... *Be in the park after the bell.*

"Why"? I asked.

"Just be there, or it'll be worse for you. She wants a fight with you," he said, with an abnormal excitement, as he pointed towards Sally, who stared right at me.

"She's going to knock the shit out of you Hattie Thompson," he said.

Looking around the classroom at the other kids, I was met with forty-one pairs of eyes, gawping back at me, waiting for my reaction.

I felt vulnerable and furious to be put under such a threat in a place where I should have been safe, but I had expected it, my instincts were spot on, so it wasn't a surprise.

"I don't want to fight. I've got to go to my Grans," I explained, with honesty. Glancing around the room, my eyes fixed on Sally, who glowered at me, punching one fist into the palm of her other hand, her lip curled in a snarl. Dad wore the same expression before he attacked us. The note didn't affect me the way Sally hoped, it prepared me, readied me to whoop her backside, but I didn't react, just held her gaze until she looked away first.

"She wants a fight with you and she's having it," Ricky Doyle reiterated, wiping his green snotty nose onto his sleeve, which almost caused me to heave. He was the most disgusting boy in our class, I sat next to him once, and he put a bogie on my ruler which made me throw up in class. Mr. Davis lost his temper and threw the board duster which hit me instead of Ricky.

"I'm going to my Gran's house, I'll miss the bus," I repeated. Gran would be worried if I didn't arrive on time. A fight would take ages, I'd be hours late, I had no idea if I would end up bloodied. I hoped not as that would upset Gran.

Ricky strode back to Sally, trying to look tough and dangerous, then strutted back to my desk, as the nasty whispering and sneaky glances started again. It overjoyed the entire class knowing there would be a fight, with me in it. Soon the whole school would know. News of fights spread like wildfire.

"She said hard luck, just be there," he shouted for the sake of the class, letting them know the fight and all arrangements involved him. There was no way out of this, though I was more than ready for her even if I didn't look like it and I would catch my bus to Grans.

When the school bell rang at four o'clock, it seemed the entire school had turned out, all crowding by the gate of the park immediately next to the school. All the kids seemed eager to watch me get thrashed. The majority were on Sally's side.

My class surrounded me as soon as I'd stepped outside of the building and frog-marched me into the park. The mob-linked arms, keeping close-knit, to prevent me from escaping, as we walked onwards.

We headed towards the park hut, its view was entirely shielded from the teacher's staff room and car park, no one would see us there.

Sally and I became encircled by hundreds of pupils from our school and neighbouring ones. Word had spread like wildfire, and the baying mobs had arrived.

Sally looked capable as she put on a show strutting around, pumping the air with her fists, imitating the boxers on TV. Her mouth was twisted as she tried to look confident and aggressive. The kids standing around chanted Sally, Sally, Sally.

I stood in position, not wanting any of this. They had forced me into it. No one cared about me. I'd have to do what I needed to do to protect myself, yet again.

As soon as Ricky the referee shouted fight, I punched Sally as hard as I could on her nose, without hesitation. My other fist came up from below and socked her on her jaw. She dropped down. It was over.

There was a silence as a few kids gathered around her, to help her get up for the next round. Her nose poured with blood; her bravado had fizzled out. She cried.

Humiliated and beaten, she ran through the park gate, shrieking. Her cocky threats had backfired. It was over, she'd lost.

The mob booed her until she was out of sight, then the bloodthirsty lot turned their attention and pride to me, as they tried to lift me up as a hero. Ricky Doyle kept praising me, having immediately changed sides, I told him to *Sod off*.

Other kids asked me about my slick technique as if they were interviewing me. I blanked them, and pushed my way through the mob, walking away slowly, to keep up appearances, then ran like mad to catch the next bus to Grans. Once onboard, I burst into tears, I'd had enough.

I told Gran what had happened, explaining the delay, she was glad I'd defended myself but upset I'd needed to.

At last, I had quashed another problem that had been worrying me for years, I'd sorted Mark Willis out, now Sally James, that still left Dad.

57 COTTON

One day, Michael and I arrived at the house to find Mum hovering by the front door looking perturbed, holding several leaflets in her hands.

Mum ushered us into the house, then showed us two receipts for airplane tickets to Russia, and brochures displaying the most magnificent buildings, a fancy hotel, and several street maps.

One receipt was in Dad's name, the other in the name of Edward Jones. Their plane was taking off as we spoke. The good thing about this was that Dad would be gone for two weeks.

"Come and see something upstairs," Mum said, causing my skin to crawl, as we followed her. Michael and I peeped in through her bedroom door, not knowing what to expect. It took us a moment to see almost invisible nylon thread, wound around Dad's bedside drawers, wardrobe, and the legs of the bed on his side, so no one could pass, nor open anything. He'd fastened it all so tightly nothing would budge.

We guessed it was to stop us from looking at his things. It also had the possibility of being a booby trap. One he wanted us to trip over. That type of nylon was sharp, I'd seen the grocer cut cheese with a similar thread.

Rather than see this as an area of prohibition, I saw it as an invitation to snoop. Dad was hiding something which needed finding, and me being a nosy, interfering busybody as I was often told, decided to investigate.

I knew Mum wouldn't look; Dad had warned her to keep away from his things. I'd heard him threaten to beat her if she went near anything of his. So, I decided I would look when Mum left to go to Gran's and Michael was at music practice.

Later that evening, I took the scissors, and within two minutes, I'd cut through every thread. It was fishing nylon; Michael had several reels of it. I'd tie it all up again later. I searched through the drawers, read his notes, and rooted through every pocket. I stopped when I found photographs of young women, pouting at the camera, or were they pouting at Dad?

All the women looked provocative and were scantily clad; they didn't look refined, like the pretty models in fashion catalogues that were delivered to our house. These ladies looked like they were selling something other than clothes and it seemed they were targeting Dad. One looked familiar, then I remembered, I'd seen her in the 'restaurant' years ago, the one Michael said was a brothel.

All the photographs had names written on; Jenny seemed to be the main one, out of the five. The young women looked about the same age, I guessed they were in their late twenties, but I couldn't be sure. The fact Dad was hiding them implied he was guilty of something bad, otherwise, he wouldn't have hidden them.

A letter dropped out from between the photographs, I'd show it to Mum later, I didn't want to read it, I'd seen enough, this wasn't for me to see, it was adult business.

I took out my stash of itching and sneezing powders I kept hidden inside my yellow cupboard in my box room, and sprinkled it into his suits, shoes, and underwear, inflicting my childish punishment on him, for his return.

I found more nylon thread, rewound what I'd cut down, then left the house, taking the evidence with me on the bus back to Gran's house. I'd give it to Mum, then she'd know what he was up to, she'd understand it all better than me.

58 JENNY AND DAD

We'd had a fabulous two weeks without Dad. We'd been able to relax and live without threat or fear. Gran had stayed a few times and enjoyed walking to the local shops. Those weeks flew by too quickly.

One evening, whilst at the house alone, someone banged on the front door, I answered to find Dad standing on the doorstep, smiling. He wasn't due back until the next day, he'd obviously changed his return flight to an earlier one.

"Hi Hattie," he said, then bounced into the house happily, as if nothing bad had ever happened. "I've got you a present," he said, pushing a bag into my hands, I glanced down to look inside, it was a furry white hat with bobbles.

"No thank you," I said, handing it back. A beautiful hat wouldn't buy my forgiveness.

He noticed two lights were switched on, one in the living room where we stood, the other in the dining area.

"Two bloody lights on, do you think I'm made of bloody money?" He yelled. He switched one light off, then went to the kitchen. I could hear him bang and clatter the pots and cupboard doors. Dad always made a noise in the kitchen, he would also sing songs in there, with lyrics of his murderous intentions and how he would spit and dance on our graves, but he didn't sing this time.

I watched him from the doorway, to make sure he didn't steal our food. For some reason, I knew he wouldn't touch me. He opened the fridge door and drank the milk out of the bottle then burped.

"That's not your milk, we bought that, do you think we're made of bloody money? Buy your bloody own!" I snarled, copying his nastiness.

He finished the last drop, glared at me defiantly, then took the bottle and smashed it in the sink, then stormed upstairs. I worried that he'd notice I'd rearranged his nylon thread.

I could hear him chanting vile abuse upstairs. It was obvious he didn't like coming back here.

The house filled again with his negative, nasty energy; I could feel the hate. He said nothing when he returned downstairs, he stormed off, out into the night, not to be seen for a week. Mum and Michael returned an hour after he left.

Mum had read the letters I'd found days ago, she refused to talk about the content in detail, only that Dad had a girlfriend.

A week later, Dad reappeared, banging the door knocker and ringing the doorbell, he'd forgotten his key. Mum opened the door, I stood behind her, Michael was at Gran's house.

Dad was standing on the doorstep with a young woman, both holding hands, with three large bags by their feet. I recognised her from the photographs, and the restaurant, it was Jenny.

They barged in and pushed past Mum and me, as Dad started to take the young woman's coat from her shoulders, both giggled like teenagers, ignoring us. We watched her wriggle out of her fake fur coat seductively, flashing her false eyelashes at my dad, as he caressed her face with the back of his hand.

"This is Jenny," he announced, brazenly, "She's moving in with me." Shock horror swept over Mum's face, at his casual announcement, as he took it for granted, she could move in.

Her bags were inside the doorway, blocking the door, three, not matching like Aunt Jane's red leather cases, just huge, tatty laundry bags, bursting at the seams, as if all her life was in them.

Dad couldn't keep still, he seemed hyper, and ecstatic as if he had arrived at a honeymoon location.

Even I could see by the way he was touching her, she was more than a friend, it was obvious he adored her. She was pretty and young. I felt sick as I thought of Mr. Burney.

I glanced at Mum, she looked devastated, I couldn't begin to imagine what was going on in her mind. The silence was deathly, as we stared at each other, I couldn't understand why someone like her would want to be with Dad, he was disgusting.

"Len, what the hell do you think you are doing. What do you take us for? Why would you do this, I'm not allowing it, I'm your wife, you have children? If you want to live with her, then leave, go on, get out. Clear off and leave us alone, take your girlfriend with you," Mum said, shakily.

We knew he didn't intend moving her in as a lodger, he would boot mum out and move this young woman in, right now. Jenny had no idea what she was letting herself in for.

Just as Mum was about to say more, Dad turned around, furious he hadn't got his own way. He looked livid. His eyes bulged. The vein in his neck twitched, then he punched Mum, full-on, knocking out another tooth and the crown. Jenny stood frozen in shock.

I screamed for them to get out, then fell on my knees to tend to Mum, who lay dazed and bleeding.

Mum dragged herself off the floor, and crawled onto a stair, holding her bloodied mouth, as she sobbed in pain and disbelief. The two lovebirds grabbed their coats and shot out through the front door, slamming it hard behind them. Immediately I opened it and called out after them; "Haven't you forgotten something?" Jenny's bags were by my feet. "Remember my Mum when he hits you; think of me and my brother, as he beats us too, you'll be next," I screamed at Dad's young girlfriend. Then I ran up the garden path and threw a bag into the garden of the thugs next door, hoping they would see Dad try to reclaim his lover's belongings. They'd go wild.

Next door's lights came on, lighting up their front garden, next their Alsatian dog barked frantically, as they thudded down the stairs. It sounded like every family member was on their way to see what was going on outside. Quickly I took the other bags and threw them out of the house. Once I'd done what I'd needed to do, I went back inside, slamming our door shut and put the lock on, then leaned back on the door, shaking with fear, as I waited for the neighbours to kick off.

Peeking through the tiny hallway window, I saw the garden next door become illuminated, as every light in their house went on. I ran upstairs to my room and continued watching the drama from my bedroom window, it was a better view from up there.

The conflict had started. I wondered if Dad dared retrieve his girlfriend's bag.

Mum came up to my room, and I asked her not to speak for a minute as I wanted to listen and watch the commotion which would soon erupt. It was payback time.

Ha! The neighbours were out now, each one psyched up and fuming, stomping around their garden, swearing and making threats, all because I'd thrown the bag onto their side of the short hedge.

"What the bloody hell are you doing in our garden?" shouted the stepfather who was bigger than Uncle Barry. He was absolutely livid.

Dad used to tell us that size didn't matter in a fight and that the bigger they are, the harder they fall, I wondered if they would fight, then I'd see if Dad's comment rang true. I doubted it.

Dad mumbled something; his voice sounded wimpish. He was almost on his knees, pleading and saying sorry, over and over, which made me laugh. Dad was a coward. I saw him walk slowly up their path, dragging the laundry bag behind him. It seemed the neighbours weren't going to let him just skulk off, as they surrounded him, and a violent din ensued, I laughed nervously, which changed rapidly to sobs. I moved away from the window and Mum held me, both of us sick of it all.

There was a lot of scuffling, swearing, and barking from the neighbour's dog, then it all became silent. I leaped out of Mum's arms and went back to watch through the window in time to see Dad and his girlfriend as they scarpered into the night; I saw their shadows disappear around the corner. The neighbours returned to their house, laughing.

Mum ran into her and dad's bedroom and searched through heaps of his clothes and eventually found another letter that read;

Oh, my beloved Lenny, sweetheart, my love, I can't wait to live with you, when they have gone. You are my life, I love you. Jenny. kisses and hugs. (Lenny & Jenny, sounds great, doesn't it?)

We hadn't been a surprise to her, she knew he had a wife and family, she didn't care about us, all she wanted was for us to get out of the house, so she could move in.

Dad turned up; he'd been gone for a month. I saw him sitting in his chair, having brought all his bad habits back with him. His snotty handkerchief was stuffed back down the side of the chair, his urine puddles soaked the toilet floor, and his rude noises stank us out. It was as if he'd never left.

It seemed his romance was over.

59 MARRIAGE ADVICE

As a last-ditched attempt to improve her marriage, Mum arranged a session with a marriage counsellor. She was still clinging on to hope and thought someone trained in failed marriages could help her, and Dad fix their broken one.

Mum refused to admit the marriage was a complete disaster and had been for a long time. We couldn't figure out how much more proof she needed to realise it was over and I couldn't understand why she'd put up with years of criminal abuse and neglect.

Mum asked Dad if he would see a psychiatrist. Her suggestion resulted in her receiving another black eye, and two more weeks off work. He did agree to see a marriage expert but only when mum's bruises had faded.

The day of the first consultation arrived, during which they met a young man who Mum later described as not being old enough to have gained any first-hand experience of life, but seemed well-read in theory.

After months of therapy, the young counsellor recommended a holiday, just for them, insisting they needed time away from the house, and distractions. He assured them their marriage would become better and stronger; it was exactly what they needed.

Michael and I listened to Mum's account of the meeting, on her lone return from the meeting. Dad had run off the moment the session ended and caught a bus headed to *'fun city'* without a word to Mum who knew where he was headed. Nothing had changed.

We thought the holiday idea, was ridiculous, we'd already given Mum the best possible advice; to leave the bully, report him to the police and get him locked up. Even as kids, we knew it was a huge risk to go anywhere with the person who wanted to kill us.

It seemed obvious Dad's violence hadn't been discussed during any of the marriage guidance meetings. We later learned dad had warned her to keep her *'trap shut,'* or else he'd *'knock the rest of her teeth out.'*

Dad agreed to the holiday. Michael and I tried to talk Mum out of going, we knew she wouldn't be safe with him, being in a country, where she didn't know anyone, and wouldn't be able to understand the language would make her more vulnerable, but she felt she had to go.

They went to Russia, it was freezing cold, the height of winter, the brochures showed people wrapped in thick coats and boots, equipped to deal with the intense elements, laughing as they sat on sleds whilst others skied down mountains, it all looked amazing. Michael and I would have loved to go there and sled, or just play in the snow and take in the incredible buildings that looked breathtaking in the brochure.

Mum had no warm clothes to take with her. To try and help her, I knitted her a long woollen scarf made of old, unravelled jumpers; It took me ten days to knit it, with a lot of help from Gran. Mum said she loved it.

I emptied the huge money bottle I used to save my money in, from returning bottles, my pocket money, and the loose change I scraped from the sides of the chairs.

My money bottle contained just over twenty pounds. I caught the bus with my pockets bulging with coins and headed to the large stores in town.

Fortunately, the sales were on, and after hours of searching, I bought Mum an imitation fur coat reduced from ninety pounds to twenty.

The day of Mum and Dad's departure to Russia had arrived, the trip of a lifetime, to reconcile a severely abusive, broken, marriage.

Michael and I waited with Mum at the bus stop for the bus to take her to the airport. She seemed optimistic and enthusiastic and told us not to worry. We felt only dread as she boarded the red double-decker bus. Mum bore a hopeful smile, as she put Gran's old suitcase, filled with the best of her worst clothes into the hold.

Michael and I waved as the bus drove away from us. Mum sat on the back seat, so she could turn and wave back until the bus turned the corner, to make a journey she should never have taken.

Dad had left earlier for reasons unbeknown to us; he said he'd meet her at the airport.

They were gone for two weeks; we had no communication with Mum during that time. Not one day passed that we didn't worry about her.

Gran came to stay with us for those two weeks, and we had fun, dancing and singing with Maggie and her sisters who would come over with bowls of stew for the three of us, they were so kind, and knew how we were suffering at the hands of Dad. Their bedroom window had a bird's-eye view into our house, they could see everything that went on here but didn't want to get involved. They had their own troubles.

The day mum returned from Russia was upsetting for all of us. She arrived in a terrible state. We could see she'd suffered, by her gaunt face, weight loss, and her nervous manner.

Mum wouldn't tell us what had happened during the trip, to fix her abusive marriage, she only wanted to tell us about the magnificent buildings and the beautiful cities.

Over time Mum told us a little of what happened; She'd found Dad at the airport, standing amidst a crowd of people in the departures lounge. It wasn't just the two of them going to reconcile their marriage, Aunt Jane, her friend Irene and another lady called Molly were going too. This wasn't a trip of reconciliation, it seemed to be something else.

Mum had a single room in the hotel, Aunt Jane and Irene, shared another, Dad and Molly had the honeymoon suite, they were having an affair and Mum was to turn a blind eye and say nothing.

Mum spent part of one day out of the two weeks with them, during which they had a photograph taken on a horse and carriage, by a tourist photographer. Dad sat with Molly on one side of the carriage, Aunt Jane, Mum, and Irene on the other.

Mum looked like she'd been crying, her face was bloated, her eyes glazed, she had obviously suffered.

The others in Dad's party must have known what was happening, but they'd chosen to do nothing to help Mum, they were the facilitators, as bad as Dad, either they'd been manipulated and brainwashed by him, or they were evil, just like him. I thought of Sally James and her followers, there was little difference.

Mum looked sad wrapped in the scarf I'd knitted for her, wearing the coat I'd bought her, the others looked happy in their long ranch mink coats and matching hats, their staged grins set in place for the camera.

Maybe they would show the photograph to the marriage counsellor. Dad would likely say Mum had been miserable all the time on the wonderful holiday. He'd make it look like she had been a killjoy, but anyone that looked closely at that photograph would see the bruises on her face and the fear in her eyes.

Maybe the expert would question who the other three women were and ask why they had gate-crashed the marriage reconciliation holiday. I doubted it.

After the staged photograph, the group walked around the beautiful streets and squares, admiring the architecture of the magnificent buildings, after an hour's sightseeing they ditched Mum back at the hotel alone, whilst they continued gallivanting.

Mum said she didn't stay in the hotel room as they'd hoped she would, she went out exploring, and walked for miles. She saw so many wonderful things and soaked up the atmosphere of Moscow until exhausted.

Dad visited Mum twice in her hotel room, she thought he wanted to talk about their problems, but on each occasion, he assaulted her in the vilest ways possible, leaving her shaken and brutally injured. She didn't see Dad or the others again until they boarded the plane. Mum sat alone, the others together chatting and laughing. It had been arranged that way.

They didn't return to the marriage counsellor, and life continued unchanged.

60 BLUE PAINT

When I was fifteen years old, I stayed at the house overnight, thinking dad was away. He stayed away often, leading his double life.

I heard a noise in the kitchen, thinking Michael had come in, I rushed downstairs to see him. When I opened the kitchen door and entered the kitchen, I saw Dad bustling around in his dressing gown. Dad looked at me strangely, then put his hand inside his dressing gown, and began moving it back and forth, as he edged towards me. It seemed he hoped to corner me.

My gut instincts were on full alert. Looking around, for something to protect myself with, I spotted a can of blue spray paint, perched on top of a cupboard. Michael had been spraying his motorbike and not put the can away. It was just within my reach. I snatched it as quickly as I could, then knocked the lid off, as Dad continued closing in on me, inch by inch, moving towards me slowly using similar tactics as the disgusting next-door neighbour Mr. Burney had when he yanked me over the gate and into his house. Luckily, I was better prepared now; I had the paint. No way was I going to be abused again.

The way the kitchen was situated meant I wouldn't have been able to escape without a struggle. Dad had positioned himself well. It was obvious; he would do something bad. My body had gone into full protection mode. Alarms rang in my head, placing me in fight mode, there was no flee option. The choices I had were; to do nothing, and suffer the consequences of his perversions, and maybe end up dead, or; do everything in my power to protect myself, my life, my everything. It was a no brainer...

Positioning the can of spray paint level with his lewd, repulsive face, I hoped with all my heart it had enough paint in to do the job I needed it to do.

"Hattie, come here," he whispered in a tone beyond sickening.

"You're always so mad at me, be nice," he said, as he continued shuffling towards me, his hand moving faster, his face bizarre. "It's time Hattie," he whispered through a mouth that had frothed; he was drooling, as he moved closer to initiate his fantasy.

I stood calm and ready; my reactions had changed from mentally hysterical to coldly calculated, I'd suddenly developed an advanced state of readiness for the worst-case scenario, and I was now faced with a nightmare that I may not get out of. Time seemed to slow down, my thoughts were clearer than ever before, as I realised, I wasn't the entertaining child that tried to save her mother and brother anymore, I was about to become something else, now I had to save myself! Now it was my turn.

It was possible I might not survive this; it was Dad's final opportunity to do what he seemed to have wanted to do for so long. I had just one chance to survive, and I couldn't waste it...

"If you come any closer, I'll spray your fucking face blue," I warned him, my voice steady and firm, my warning clear. He dismissed my words with a shake of his head and continued to shuffle towards me as his hand went hell for leather, beneath the dressing gown, the one mum bought him to salvage some decency which he didn't have. Dad wouldn't stop. He looked determined to carry his desires to a level of no return. This could end badly, hopefully for him, not me. He should have believed I would carry out my threat, he should have moved back, and left me alone, but no, he had to keep on, with the same wry smile and twinkling eyes leering at me perversely. "Shush, don't be so silly Hattie," he laughed heinously, as he made a slight move towards me, his hand still moving rapidly, his gown now open. "You're always bloody fussing Hattie, stop being so silly, you're such a busybody, a little know it all, but that's ok, come here now, silly girl." Dad's face and tone knocked me sick.

"You're a disgrace!" I told him, as I pressed my finger down hard, and sprayed the paint. I watched the blue paint, squirt out like a geyser, covering his glasses, his face, his open sloppy mouth, and into and over his nostrils. I pressed so hard on the nozzle that it felt like it had gone through my thumb. My hand continued moving the can up and down with speed, as his hands tried to shield his face. I continued spraying until there was nothing left in the can.

Under the paint, Dad's face looked horrified, he'd stopped dead in his tracks, his open mouth now a bright shade of metallic blue, outside and in. His oral froth had mixed with the paint. He attempted to shout at me, regretting it immediately as his lips spluttered blue paint, and he didn't dare swallow.

Hysterical laughter bubbled within me, a mixture of nerves, fear, and relief that I'd protected myself, but I wasn't sure if I was out of danger just yet.

Dad was in a state of bewildered panic. His glasses had slipped down his nose and onto the floor. Instinctively he opened his eyes for a split second, then immediately closed them, as the paint dribbled in off his eyelashes and I squirted some more, managing to get a couple of decent squirts out of the can. His rude hands rubbed his lewd eyes frantically, making things much worse for himself.

I'd given Dad a taste of his own medicine and he didn't seem to like it. I shoved him out of my way as he fumbled, he looked pathetic and helpless, he'd made Mum helpless when he beat her, now the tables had turned. His blue-painted glasses were on the floor, my foot crunched down on them. Dad started to scream wildly. I wasn't sure if I'd hurt him, or if he was having a tantrum, I didn't care.

Leaving him screaming I made it out through the front door, and I ran, as fast as my legs would carry me. My energy soared, fuelled by my adrenaline. I wondered if he'd call the police, I hoped he would, then I would tell them everything the monster had done to us for years, no doubt he would get a prison sentence, as I'd read about people who had done even less than he had, and they had been sent down for a long time.

When I arrived at Gran's house, I found Mum clipping the hedge, in the front garden, she took one look at me and took me straight into the house to sit me down, where I told her what had happened, Gran stood by the door listening, both were horrified.

"Gran, please can I live with you permanently? I don't want to go near him ever again," I gulped, still in shock. Gran stretched her frail arms out to me and hugged me as only a grandma could. "Of course, you can, Hattie, you stay with me as long as you like, you know that already. We'll look after each other. Helen, the same goes for you and Michael."

Though safe now, and happy, I couldn't stop worrying about Mum and Michael, nor could I understand why they hadn't accepted Gran's offer of a home. They were still living in that horrid house, with him, when they didn't need to. They had a place here, with us.

61 BROTHER'S 18th BIRTHDAY

It was Michael's eighteenth birthday. The day he became an adult. It was tragic his childhood had been destroyed, written off in a turmoil of constant, methodical physical, and mental abuse. Most families would celebrate this special day with a huge party, but for Michael, there were no family celebrations. Sadly, this day turned out to be one of the worst days of his life.

Michael let me go with him to his friend's house, after which we returned to the house, to collect his trumpet, intending to ride back to Gran's house on his motorbike. On our return, Michael tried his key several times in the front door, the lock wouldn't turn, it felt reminiscent of the time we'd been burgled. He knocked on the door umpteen times, Dad didn't come to open it, even though he knew we were there. I'd seen the curtain twitch in the little window, by the front door, he'd no doubt been peeping at us ever since we arrived, and seemed adamant he wasn't letting us in.

It was late; we wanted to get into the house. Michael still lived here, and it was within our rights to be there. Michael wanted to collect his trumpet and leave immediately; it would take two minutes at most. "He's being awkward again," Michael said, forlornly. I looked at my brother, he was so handsome, it broke my heart to look at him, as flashbacks of seeing him beaten came into my mind. He was eighteen today, the least Dad could do was let him in on his birthday.

We continued banging louder, causing a commotion, determined to go in, get the trumpet, then leave. I could see neighbour's curtains twitching, lights went on, a few people had come out onto their doorsteps to see what the din was all about. We stood by the door for over twenty minutes, waiting and shivering in the torrential rain, with the wind howling, both of us soaking wet in the dreadful March winds.

"Dad won't let us in and it's Michael's birthday, and dad's being awkward" I shouted out to two locals standing by our gate, their large umbrellas had blown inside out, by the harsh wind, "He's eighteen today, and Dads changed the locks on his birthday," I added hysterically. Tears streamed down my face already drenched by the rain.

The couple by our gate stared at the closed house without expression or emotion; like ghouls, only their nosey curiosity kept them in place.

Dad opened the door, mad as hell, then stood on the step, blocking entry into the house, yelling at Michael and me... "You don't bloody well live here anymore, just get your things, and piss off."

The ghouls by our gate watched on with interest. I saw they were standing on the tips of their toes; their faces had livened up a little. The street lamp lit up their faces, displaying their morbid curiosity. This was a wonderful source of entertainment for them, a bit of excitement to liven up their boring lives and give them something to gossip about, to us it was devastating.

Eventually, Dad let us in, Michael went to his bedroom, at the end of the landing, to get his trumpet, as I watched and waited on the landing, where I could look downstairs to check on Dad's whereabouts. Dad remained downstairs, prancing back and forth in the hallway, he seemed agitated. He looked upwards, for us, as I glared at him from above to be met with a face of rage.

The tension building up was tangible, rising to a terrifying degree; We needed to get out of there damned quick. "Hurry Michael, come on, we need to go," I urged, something would go off, I could feel it. The atmosphere felt strained.

There was a key on the top of the banister, hoping it was a spare for the new lock, I shoved it into my pocket then I paced the length of the landing, sneaking glances downstairs to check on Dad but he was nowhere to be seen, so I moved towards Michael's room, to see if I could do anything to help.

Without warning, Dad was upstairs; he'd moved so fast it took me by surprise. Dad barged into me, knocking me out of his way as he charged towards Michael's room. I wasn't able to warn Michael in time as I'd been winded and was down on the floor. As soon as I recovered, I flew to Michael's room, sadly, seconds too late.

Dad pounced on Michael like a seasoned rugby player. I knew he would inflict as much damage and injury to Michael as he could. Like all the other times, he'd taken Michael unawares, that was how Dad worked; cowardly, taking his time, waiting for the innocent to be distracted, then he'd pounce.

Dad looked insane, but he wasn't, he knew what he was doing, he liked it. Dad was evil, cruel, and jealous, of his own son, his own flesh, and blood. It felt like the end was nigh as the threats and swearing spewed out of his foul mouth. Michael was shouting for Dad to let go as he was dragged out of his bedroom by his hair. He couldn't do anything to get out of the hold even though he tried hard to retaliate.

It was chaotic, as Dad tugged my brother and lashed out at him with his clenched fists. Michael tried to fight Dad off, his legs clung onto the architrave of the door, as his arms tried to grab dad's legs to pull him down, but it was impossible to save himself.

I tried pulling Dad's jumper from the back, wanting to inflict the same punishment I gave him years ago, but I couldn't get near him, his anger was at a higher level, he was on his mission.

Dragging Michael into the small toilet room, my heart pounded with absolute dread of what was to come in that horrid tiny room where he used to pretend to photograph me, through the top glass window, where I sat petrified, as the flash on his camera went off; all I could do was stare at the door and panic as he rattled the doorknob calling out in a sleazy tone; "Hattie, darling Hattie, can I come in," pleading to be let into a room that should have been safe, and private. Now he's dragged my brother into what would become a torture chamber and I can't get close enough to help.

Dad screeched profanities, psyching himself up for his grand finale, against my brother, the prize he'd never truly conquered. I saw how he knocked Michael's head against the wall, punched him, kicked him, then rammed his head between the toilet basin and the brick wall, pulverizing him, until he lay unconscious, and I felt terrible that I couldn't do enough to stop Dad, everything was happening too fast, I couldn't get in to help him. Michael hadn't stood a chance; he'd been caught unawares. I threw myself, at Dad, trying to knock him away, screaming for him to stop, but he continued to wade in, even though Michael was out cold.

This time, Dad was going for the kill, regardless of the consequences, he lashed out furiously, his ramblings incoherent. My brother seemed lifeless, yet Dad continued punching him because today he was a man and not a little boy. "Leave him alone, you've killed him, you've killed him!" I screamed, but my screaming wasn't going to stop him.

Everyone down our road must have heard the din. The neighbours at the top of the path did nothing; no one came to investigate the loud screams coming from the house, no one called the police, nobody cared.

Dad knew Michael was unconscious, his body was limp, it was as if Dad was beating a corpse. "Somebody call the police, please call the police," I screamed, no one did, why weren't the people at the top of the path helping? I couldn't understand.

Hanging off Dad's back, I tried pulling his hair with all my might to rip it out of his scalp, desperate to stop him, to no avail. Dad elbowed me in the ribs and I had to let go, as the pain ripped through me. My mission was to save Michael; he was running out of time. Thankfully, he was alive, I heard a groan, as Dad sneaked a hard kick into his side, but he could do nothing, other than feel it.

Gathering every ounce of energy and defensiveness to the core of my being, I leaped onto dad's back and sunk my fingers into his face. I tried cow biting him, from behind. Dad elbowed me hard, in my stomach again. "Hattie, stop, or you'll get a beating too," he threatened, as I writhed in agony.

Dad slowed down; only because he was wheezing. He looked bizarrely at my motionless brother, assessing where to strike him next as if seeking the place that would inflict the most pain and damage.

Charging downstairs, I frantically ran through the house, in search of anything that would help me get Dad off Michael, who would not survive any more beatings. We were losing time, Dad didn't care if he killed either of us, he was too far gone, he looked perverse and deliriously happy.

There was no more paint to spray on him, but I spotted Dad's umbrella hung on the end of the banister, I grabbed it, unsure of what I could do with it, then ran back upstairs as fast as I could, and piled into another battle as my adrenaline soared and my heart almost burst with the speed and intensity only absolute panic can bring. Immediately, I hit Dad over the head with his old-fashioned umbrella, taking him by surprise. *`Come on, Hattie, you must do this, you need to save your brother, don't look down at him, focus on Dad, `* I told myself. I had to get him away from Michael, who could die, and it seemed Dad wanted him dead. I couldn't shift the cowardly brute, no matter how hard I hit out or poked him. His adrenaline was soaring through his body so fast; he didn't seem to register anything I did. I needed to use more force and hit harder if that were possible, I wasn't holding back, but it was far from enough.

I looked at my poor brother, out cold, on the floor, incapacitated by the man who should have loved him. My heart was broken.

Dad gave me the strangest lustful leer, it was perverse. He looked ecstatic as he watched me fight to save my sibling with vigour; I was entertaining him or fulfilling a sick fantasy. I knew he could have easily slung me out of his way, but he enjoyed my being there. Another thought occurred to me; Perhaps I reminded him of his sister, Aunt Jane and he was doing to us, what his father had done to them, and now he was trying to finish us off, where his father had failed. All thoughts ran through my chaotic mind as I automatically tried to make sense of this madness... Did Aunt Jane not try to help him when he was Michael's age, when his father beat the hell out of him, was that why she gave him all that money, to ease her guilt? But if she was a terrified child, then she had nothing to feel guilty about.

My thoughts continued as if separate from my body... I stood and walked behind Dad. Pushed the umbrella's hook past his neck, then dropped backwards. The hook latched onto his throat. Immediately I yanked at the umbrella's handle with all the strength I could muster. With one hand grasping the handle, my other hand flew over his greasy head and onto his face. Frantically, I dug my nails deep into the flesh of his cheeks at the same time, I dragged him by his neck and began my descent down the stairs, pulling him off balance, away from my brother, as Dad squealed with pain. If he leaned back further, we'd tumble down the stairs, if he leaned forward, he'd asphyxiate, if I let go, he'd probably kill me. Maintaining my grip on the umbrella, I prevented him from punching Michael.

The bully continued punching the air with one fist, whilst his free hand tugged the hook at his neck until he lost his balance. As Dad wobbled, I stepped down a step to get out of his way, in case he fell on me. He recognized his dilemma.

There were sixteen steps, I was down three. I'd leap backwards and take the bully down by his neck, I'd do anything to stop him from killing Michael. "Promise you'll stop," I shouted, as I adjusted the hook's pressure to his detriment. He wouldn't stop, so I continued my descent, adding to the pressure. It was working, Dad was having to step back to follow my lead down the stairs. He was away from Michael now and busily fumbling with the hook that dug into his throat.

Dad wheezed profusely. He raised his hand, like a white flag, to signal he was giving in as he struggled to breathe. Tears streamed down my face as I prepared myself to leap down the remaining stairs if he started again. Dad rasped in a weak voice... "All right, all right, stop, that's enough." Slackening my hold, I thought better of it and tugged once more on the hook as hard as I possibly could, to let him know I still had control.

Gripping his throat, Dad lay sprawled across the stairs. I released my hold of the umbrella and stepped over him to get to Michael. It was only my self-restraint that prevented me from kicking Dad in the face and down the stairs.

Seconds later, Dad got up and scurried to his bedroom as I picked up the umbrella and jabbed him once more in the neck. I wasn't scared to leap in and fight, I was ready to go again, my adrenaline was sky high, my confidence soaring. "You bitch," he mumbled, as he skulked off, gasping for his inhaler. If it hadn't been for his bronchitis, I doubted I could have stopped him, thankfully, his weakness, had been my strength, that, or knowing he could have easily killed me, but I'd never been Dad's target, his targets were Mum and Michael.

My priority now was to help my brother. I needed to act quickly before Dad returned to get the last boot in. With difficulty, I eased Michael's head from the vice between the toilet basin and wall needing to get him out of there. He was unconscious and immediate medical attention was necessary, but I was the only one who could help. Sitting on the floor, I held him in my arms and checked his ears for bleeding, a sign that Mum had warned us about if he ever bumped his head. Michael suffered a hairline fracture to his skull years ago, a terrible incident, I knew nothing about until recently. Bleeding ears would have been a terrible sign.

There were so many vicious assaults I would be told about, over time, many I'd not witnessed, others I'd buried in the depths of my memory, and those that Mum documented in diaries. All would be revealed, in the future. No way would Dad get away with what he had done, nor his accomplices, of which there were many.

I sat for a long time, resting Michael's head on my lap, shaking as the reality of what had happened sank in. The thoughts of having witnessed Michael fighting for his life with such vigour and desperation overwhelmed me, I couldn't understand any of it. Stroking Michael's cheeks, I whispered through my tears, "I love you, Michael, we're leaving soon." Though I had no idea how we'd make it through the door. It wasn't clear what Dad intended to do next, all I knew was we needed to get out of the house, pretty damn quick.

Thankfully, I heard the door slam. It was Dad, running off into the night, I wondered what he told the nosey gossips at the top of our path on his way out. I visualized him laughing it off, saying; "Oh, kids, they're a bloody nuisance, always fighting, they make a heck of a noise," making light of yet another attempted murder, he'd done that for years, been the assailant, the criminal, whilst we, the victims were ignored, or made to look like the guilty ones.

Using my jumper as a pillow, I lay it under Michael's head, while I got some water to wet his face to try to bring him around, telling him, "I love you, Michael, you are the best brother in the world, please be all right, please."

I was scared Dad would return. My throat was raw from screaming, like so many times before.

"Come on Michael, please wake up." I didn't know if he would, I needed to wait. After several minutes, he came around; "Stay with me Michael," I whispered, holding him in my arms. He lay still for twenty minutes, as I rocked him like a babe in arms, unable to imagine how he felt.

He mumbled, asking for water, that was a good sign. Moments later, I helped him onto his feet, his legs immediately gave way, he said he felt dizzy and his head ached badly, yet he managed to ask if I was all right and if Dad had done anything to me.

Those dizzy episodes and headaches from this beating and so many others would last Michael a lifetime.

"Why us, what did we do?" I kept asking myself as I held onto Michael, we were good people, Mum was lovely, Michael was a great son, a fantastic brother, he was compassionate, a gentleman with impeccable manners, he'd make a wonderful husband and a fabulous Dad, he would be nothing like ours and I would be nothing like Aunt Jane, I knew it.

Michael leaned on me for support as we hobbled around the house, trying to regain his balance. We both knew we had to leave immediately. There was only Michael's motorbike to escape on. It didn't seem like a safe option but it was the only one we could take. "I think in half an hour I may feel able to take us to Gran's," Michael told me. "What if Dad comes back?" I asked. Just as I mentioned him, we heard a key turn in the lock, our hearts sank, both of us scared he'd returned to kill us.

Dad peeped through the living room door where he was met with my terrified face looking back at him; he disappeared upstairs. We didn't dare wait any longer for Michael to recover, we needed to go. Holding hands, we sneaked out through the back door quietly, making our way into the alley, another place that terrified me. The place where Mr. Burney abducted me.

The cold wind and heavy rain livened Michael up. The desperate need to get away energized him, as together we pushed the heavy motorbike out of the ginnel, and onto the road. Silently, we headed towards the next block of houses. Only when we were hidden from view did we get on, and Michael start the engine.

Looking back towards the house, from a safe distance we saw the unhelpful gossips by our gate stood like zombies under a broken umbrella in the torrential rain. Both seemed fascinated by the commotion. They knew a young man had been beaten to an inch of his life in the house. They had heard our screams for help and did nothing. It seemed they had no idea we'd sneaked out of Dad's house; they were probably waiting for the next round of abuse to kick off.

Michael pressed down hard on the accelerator, and we rode off, making our escape towards safety. I held onto Michael's waist, sobbing my heart out, leaving our nightmares behind us. We never saw Dad again.

62 WHITE PLASTIC BAGS

Two months passed, since that awful night when we rode away on Michael's motorbike, beaten and traumatised on his eighteenth birthday. Thankfully Mum moved in with Gran, Michael, and me.

A few weeks later, we received a letter from Dad;

Helen,

There are several bags for collection. If you can let me know the time, and the day you can come for them, then I can arrange for someone to be here to let you in. Len.

Mum wrote back, giving a time and date to collect our belongings I went along with her in her second-hand car. Audrey let us into the house and took us into Michael's old bedroom and pointed to a row of little white plastic bags, in a line across the floor. They contained our belongings. Audrey stood to attention by the door, watching us as if she were a security guard.

Someone had removed the furniture. All that was left to show for our existence in this dump, were the bags. Mum and I wanted to get out as soon as possible, as the atmosphere and memories were sickening.

The smell of fresh paint and noises downstairs had us guessing decorators were in the house. We knew for sure it wouldn't be Dad, his breathing would suffer too much and he was useless at decorating, he didn't have the skill or the patience.

Both Mum and I felt like trespassers with Audrey glaring at us, keeping us confined to one room. We'd wanted to go to each room for our belongings as Mum had items of value she needed to ensure had not been overlooked during the packing of the bags. Audrey looked unapproachable. She was obviously under orders; it was pointless saying anything to her.

We packed the little white bags into the boot of the car, still curious about the coin and car collections, that didn't appear to have been packed, the bags weren't heavy enough or full enough to contain the amount Mum and Michael had. Pop had entrusted Michael with the vintage cars on the premise he'd pass them down to future generations or sell them in times of need, as they were the originals and would only increase in value, over time.

It seemed Audrey was Dad's housekeeper now. I was surprised as I'd learned her ex-husband had been as violent and as bad as my dad. I wondered why she would divorce one bully to look after yet another? It made little sense, not unless there was money involved.

We drove away with the car full to the brim with what we knew was junk and passed several neighbours who used to be friendly, now their backs were turned against us. We'd done nothing wrong. We were the victims. It seemed obvious, Dad had spread lies about us and everyone believed them.

Once out of sight, I switched the radio on full blast and opened the window to let the fresh air in. Mum and I sang and laughed at the top of our voices. Glad to be free, and safe.

Back at Gran's house, we checked through the bags. It was as we'd suspected; the coins and vintage toy cars were missing; they had left us with junk which we put straight into the bin." Mum looked at Michael and me and said; "Never mind, they're only things, I'm lucky, I have everything, I have my children."

63 BACK TO COLLECT

Several months after we'd moved in with Gran, I returned to Dad's house, to search for, and if successful, reclaim Michael's vintage model car collection, and Mum's coins. Dad had no right to keep them.

No one knew I'd taken the spare door key that dreadful night on Michael's eighteenth birthday. Not only did I want to take what was ours, but I also wanted to see what the house was like now.

Placing a large shopping bag onto my shoulder and the lead on Fred, my Labrador. I set off on my Mission, terrified, but determined.

Fred would guard me against any threat Dad may make, he was a great deterrent and protector; he'd proved himself when I got accosted in the park during what I'd hoped would be a pleasant walk. It seemed the flashers had now taken over the local park. Fred stopped the evil intended for me, by pinning the flasher against a tree, until the police arrived. Moments later, they took the threat away in their van.

A lady I knew gave Fred to me, as he was too boisterous for her, but he calmed down with exercise training and belly rubs. Within two weeks, he did everything I taught him to do, understanding my tone of voice, and many of my hand commands.

Fred and I arrived at Dad's house. After ensuring no one was in, I opened the door, took a deep breath, and forced myself to enter the sad, angry house.

... Memories of me aged seven, stood in the hallway, my ear to the door, terrified, in my yellow dress flashed through my mind. I shook the memory from my mind. I had to move forward and do what I came here to do, collect our belongings then leave, as fast as I could.

With Fred at my heel, we went walkabout, stunned at what I saw. It seemed everywhere had been decorated expensively and furnished with great style. I thought we were poor; I said to myself. This made cousin Katie's house look shabby.

Someone had painted the walls in the latest ivory silk, non-drip paint. It created an illusion of the small hallway and stairwell looking large.

All the doors had gold shiny handles that matched the light switches and sockets. Gone were the old sticky plastic ones with paint dribbling down, in the most disgusting, pink paint Dad had scrounged from the council.

It was no wonder dad could afford all this; he had spent nothing on us, or the house, in the twenty years since Mum and Dad first moved in.

It seemed obvious he'd had interior designers put this look together, and professional decorators paint and hang the wallpaper. Dad couldn't have done this himself.

I remembered his attempt at hanging wallpaper. A memory I'd long since forgotten; I'd been about four years old, holding a brush for him in case he needed it, as he hung soggy wallpaper onto the bathroom walls. It kept ripping as he tried to flatten the air bubbles with his bare hands.

The paper didn't fit the wall; it was a foot too short. Dad got so angry he picked up the bucket of lumpy wallpaper paste and threw it across the bathroom.

Dad shouted as if he was in pain, then tore the dark wallpaper with fish patterns, off the wall. The dreary paper rolled down onto his head. He was furious. I became hysterical with the giggles because he looked so funny with the paper draped over his face. He kept spluttering as the paste had gone into his mouth. When I realised, he was furious and not playing, I screamed in confusion and horror. Dad ran out of the house raging, leaving Mum to placate me and clean up his mess.

I continued walking through the house, wondering how many more horrid memories would return.

In the hallway, I saw the large space under the stairs was now a cloakroom with sliding doors. it had been an open space, where we hung damp, dirty coats in piles. Our smelly garments were mouldy due to the damp weather we always had and the damp house where they never dried. Dad hung several work jackets here. I'd root through the pockets to claim our pocket money, of half a crown each, per week. We didn't dare ask him for it. That was too risky. He'd promised it to us, so I took it, to avoid him smashing the house up and beating us, as he was prone to do.

The arrangement had been to ask him for our spends every Friday evening. The first time we asked, he ripped his shirt off his own back with both hands; the buttons pinged across the room, his face went bright red, his eyes bulged from their sockets, and he picked up the poker and chased us around the house threatening to beat us to a pulp, screaming the money was only his.

Michael caught me one Friday evening with my hand deep down into Dad's jacket pocket claiming our pocket money; Dad was asleep.

"You're stealing, Hattie," Michael warned me. "He'll kill you if he catches you."

"No, I'm not stealing. Dad said we could have it. He promised us, so I'm taking what he said we could have."

64 THE LIVING ROOM

I walked into the living room. It was unrecognizable. A chandelier took pride of place in the middle of the ceiling with a plaster rose behind it, making it look even more ornate. Plaster coving finished the look, which continued through to the dining area. It seemed the dump we'd lived in had been transformed into a palace.

An enormous, soft, cream leather suite fitted the living room perfectly, replacing the old, ripped plastic mustard settee and the two shabby chairs. I'd seen this suite advertised on television. One could press a button to recline, press another and a footstool emerged from beneath.

A large colour television set dominated the corner where our old black and white one used to be, the one we had to thump to get it to work, almost punishing it to make the picture stop spinning. This one had a remote control, so Dad wouldn't need to move from his comfy leather recliner.

Visions of Mum screaming in agony, shielding her face from the beatings in the same spot as the television flashed through my mind.

The carpeting was an attention grabber; it matched throughout the house. No more frayed end of the roll, mismatched pieces tacked down with rusty nails. This was thick, plush, and patterned, with no sign of joins or lumps. A professional had laid this, it fitted perfectly.

The fluff from the carpet floated up, as I walked through the house, with Fred by my side. It wouldn't do Dad's breathing any good.

Fred made himself busy rolling and digging into the thick wool pile with his claws, then chased the fluff, catching it in his snout.

I remembered the carpet burns on my knees as Dad flung me face down on the old nylon rug.

A gorgeous new top-of-the-range gas fire was set within a new marble fireplace, giving the room an ambiance of romance, to a luxurious abode that was once a scruffy dump. I could still see the violence that took place here and still feel the eeriness of hate and despair. The fear on my loved one's faces and our desperation remained in this evil contaminated house, it was tangible. Dad couldn't paint away our suffering no matter how much expensive paint he bought. I hoped the memories tormented him.

I wondered what Aunt Sarah and cousin Katie would think now, no doubt they would be impressed, perhaps even jealous.

65 DINING ROOM

The dining room looked exquisite, too good for Dad's atrocious table manners. I remembered the *brothel restaurant* we went to with Dad, on the pretense it was a *works do*. I was too young to understand then, but I understood it now. It seemed this decorated dining room wasn't for Dad to dine alone in. It was to entertain women like Jenny.

I remembered how Dad used to sit at the old table with a wonky leg, occasionally dining with us. He would burp, pick his teeth with wooden toothpicks that flirted his chewed meat across the table. He'd scraped at his plate with his knife until the pattern almost came off. We'd all felt nauseous as he'd talked with his food rotating in his open mouth.

When his belly was full, he'd belch long and hard, and never excuse himself. After which he'd take out his disgusting cloth handkerchief, which had been used over several days, open it, and shake it as if performing magic, I'd expected a rabbit to pop out as he shook his germs at us. He'd rub his mouth, blow his nose, find a dry section of his handkerchief, fold it over and put it back into his bacteria-laden pocket. After he'd rubbed his full belly, he'd flop into his chair, hog the fire and block the television from our view, while he broke wind all evening, then sleep.

Another terrible memory, returned, one of our budgie Benny. My eyes filled with tears as I recalled our beautiful, blue tiny friend. Our first and only pet. I remembered we were sat at the table eating fish and chips. Benny was loose. He used to sit on the edge of our plates and nibble the fish batter. For no reason, Dad punched him hard, knocking him off the table and right across the room. We ran to him and saw him panting in a tiny mound. His beak had been punched skew-whiff, and his tiny heart was beating so fast.

Mum scooped our little budgie up into her shaking hands and tried to help him as Michael and I looked on horrified. We saw Benny die in Mum's hands, as the three of us cried for yet another innocent victim of Dad's brutality.

Overcome with sadness and memories of evil doings, I continued making my way around the house, facing my demons. I had to do this if I was to move on with my life. I needed to understand what had happened here, I needed answers as to why we had been so badly treated when we'd done nothing wrong. It was doubtful I would find any. Nothing could explain Dad's cruelty, apart from the fact he was an evil, cruel bully who enjoyed hurting the weak.

66 THE BATHROOM

I paused by the bathroom at the top of the stairs, as the sick memories returned and I recalled my fears. This was another room where I'd been terrified, one in which Dad tormented me from the other side of the door.

Forcing myself to enter I found the dirty room had been changed beyond recognition. There was a pearl corner bath, with gold taps. I switched one on, to find automatic hot water pouring out. We'd had to wait hours for the water to get warm in the boiler when we lived here, then it would trickle out of the tap as Dad didn't know how to renew the washers.

I remembered how we used to share the same bathwater on Sundays. It was always me who was the last one to get into the filthy cold water full of hair and scum.

I hated Sunday bath night. I felt dirtier getting out of the bath than I had when I got in. Sometimes the bathwater would have green perfumed crystals in, which gave me an allergic rash and I'd stink of chemicals for days, until the next bath night, a week later.

It had been my job to empty the water when I'd finished, I had to scrub the scum off the sides with white scouring powder that burned my fingers.

I'd remove the hair from the plughole which smelled like rotten eggs, which knocked me sick, and I'd vomit into the washbasin next to the bath.

Mum said she would clean the bath, telling Dad it wasn't a job for a little child to do, but he insisted I did it. I was five years old the first time I cleaned that bath out.

The bathroom wall had been knocked through into the tiny room that housed the toilet. The airing cupboard had gone. All the walls had ivory and mirrored tiles, creating a fantastic, light, space, giving the illusion of it being twice its size, just like Katie's bedroom.

It looked too good for Dad, as his bathroom habits had always been appalling, no doubt he'd still pollute the air and miss his aim. The pretty mat by the toilet wouldn't stay ivory coloured for long, no matter how much money he spent on it.

The fear I'd felt so many times growing up in this house, came flooding back, as the haunting memories of Dad loitering by the bathroom door, breathing heavily, whispering my name returned; First, he would make sure no one was around to witness his sick game. Once he'd ascertained he was in the clear, he'd switch the landing, bathroom, and toilet lights off, after flickering them for a while to scare me. The switches were outside the rooms so he had full control.

Dad would have his camera with him and he'd set off the flash at the glass pane at the top of the bathroom and toilet doors. I didn't know if he was taking photographs of me or pretending to. I was so scared that I couldn't move.

When I was in the bath, Dad would rattle the doorknob, bang, tap, and scratch the door as I lay rigid in the water. I'd sink so low only my nostrils remained above the water level. I lay, terrified of drowning and even more petrified he would come in.

Other times, I would hide in the airing cupboard, where I burned myself on the uncovered, copper boiler, there wasn't enough space for me in there, so I'd squeeze in regardless, hoping he couldn't see me hiding, as I had when Mr. Burney abducted me. Dad showed concern when that happened, yet he put me in the same situation, so many times. Why would he do that? how could he have been so cruel? I knew I would never find the answers, but I would seek revenge, no one should get away with what he'd done, people went to prison for less, I read about them in the papers, daily.

67 PARENT'S ROOM

Taking a deep breath, I went into Mum's bedroom, the room she'd shared with Dad. Another room which had been vandalised by the burglars and the place where Dad assaulted Mum viciously, so many times.

This was where Michael had to beat Dad off mum with a walking stick, to make him stop yet another evil assault, as Mum lay in bed screaming. I'd been at Gran's, but I'd seen the state Mum was in later when I returned to the house. I saw how upset Michael was, as he told me what happened, without going into details but I guessed correctly.

This was the room where I went to collect Mum's valuable watch she had hidden, which she needed to sell as we were struggling to buy basic provisions because Dad wouldn't give her any housekeeping money. I'd tapped gently on the door so I wouldn't disturb Dad, but he was awake...

"Come on in Hattie, it's ok, come on," he'd called. I opened the door only to find he was lying in bed, acting strangely. Dad's hand was under the sheet moving up and down. His eyes ogled me. A wry smile quivered on his thin-lipped mouth, as his hand pumped wildly beneath the sheets, and his breathing sounded as if he was having an asthmatic attack.

I retreated as quickly as I could, shaken. This happened a week before I sprayed him with the blue paint.

After the paint incident, I told Mum of the other times he'd exposed himself and other lewd acts. Mum immediately filed for a divorce. I wished she'd filed sooner.

At last, we had protection. Mum cited Dad for physical, mental, and sexual abuse towards all of us.

Dad signed the Divorce papers which listed his inappropriate, lewd, violent behavior which Dad confirmed was correct.

He made a request to the courts to have access to me, but regardless of what was agreed, he'd never have it. I refused to have anything to do with him, as did Michael, and Mum. The rest of the extended family remained loyal to him. As far as we were concerned, using Dad's terminology; *They bloody well deserved each other.*

68 FRED'S IN THE HOTHOUSE

Today was Thursday, Dad would be at night school, teaching until 10 pm. He usually went to an adult club afterward. I knew that because an old school friend whom I bumped into one day whilst shopping told me she worked in that club as a barmaid. She filled me in on Dad's disgusting behaviour, telling me how he pestered the younger women, sometimes he'd go off with one or two of them, and return hours later, looking quite flushed.

To prepare for his return, I made his palatial house warm as it was freezing cold outside. We'd never known the house to be warm. We had to put extra layers of coats on, or sit by the one bar radiator when it was cold. Sometimes we'd share a perished hot rubber water bottle and hope it didn't burst.

Now, Dad had a splendid gas fire which I switched to its highest setting. The rapid, intense heat, soon warmed the room. I closed the doors, as Dad had trained us all to do, so the heat couldn't escape, remembering how Dad would shout if one of us left the door open; "It costs bloody money to heat this bleeding house," he'd yell, as we shivered. Closing the door made no difference.

Whilst the house was warming up. I continued my tour. Upon entering the kitchen, my attention veered to a huge, deluxe fridge freezer. Curiosity got the better of me as I opened the door to see what he ate, now we had gone.

Our tiny fridge when we lived here had housed milk, cheese, spam, and offal from the market, I saw none of these foods here now.

To my surprise, Dad had stocked the fridge and freezer with many interesting delicacies. I saw two large jars of Beluga caviar perched on the top shelf, a stock of smoked salmon, quail, and other wonderful edibles filled the other shelves. I assumed the caviar must have been a gift from someone with lots of money, perhaps someone from Russia as the label had what looked like Russian writing on it. I knew Dad wouldn't have bought them; he was too tight.

It didn't matter where the food came from; it was his job to feed me until I was eighteen that was the Law. He'd agreed to abide by it, not that he had much choice.

I'd read about Beluga caviar in a magazine. Celebrities and rich people ate it at exclusive events and expensive restaurants, according to the magazines. We would never have been able to afford any of it.

This was one of the best caviar's in the world, which was hardly surprising, as he'd always namedropped and moved in circles where money was no object.

"Oh my," I said to Fred. "This must be the ultimate in caviar. I wonder how much it costs, but if I have to ask the price, then I can't afford it."

Fred was sitting by my feet, looking at me. "Oh, I forgot to tell you, Fred, we're poor, Katie told me a long time ago, so it will be a cheap imitation. It won't upset Daddy in the slightest when he sees it's all gone."

Piling a teaspoon high with luscious caviar, I put it into my mouth to try, then spat it out. "Oh dear, I don't like it, Fred. It's not what it's all cracked up to be," I said, imitating cousin Katie.

I tipped the jar's contents onto the new, polished parquet flooring, which had replaced the old linoleum, feeling rather mischievous.

Fred was excited, waiting on his best behaviour, sitting up straight, eager to try it.

On my command, he stood up, waited for me to tell him he could eat, then he gobbled down the expensive caviar. His tail wagged with delight. I continued praising him as I tipped out the contents of the second jar.

Fred licked his lips, enjoying his high-priced treat that even the rich would only eat on rare occasions and in lesser quantities.

As I continued, tears poured down my cheeks. I lay on the floor, sobbing as I recalled the terrible ways in which Dad had abused us, and deprived us of the most basic of necessities which we didn't dare ask for, whilst he indulged himself, rewarding himself for being a tyrant at our expense. All the suffering we'd endured, the misery, pain, and the fear, was all too much. I sobbed until exhausted as Fred tried to lick me. He put his paw on me, seeming to understand my distress wanting to make things right for me, comfort, and protect me. I hugged him until I stopped crying, then continued my search as I tried to make sense of it all.

Our only crime had been our existence. We'd been the unwanted hindrance who impeded Dad's debauchery. We were his conscience; which he didn't want to awaken.

I didn't find the car collection or the coins, but at least I'd tried, I'd looked everywhere.

I put Fred on his lead, ready to leave the sweltering house of horrors, but first I had a few jobs to do.

The three chandeliers held fifteen bulbs each, I switched them all on. As I walked around each room, I switched all the lamps, heaters, and fans on then unplugged the fridge and freezer.

Dad didn't like us using over five inches of water in the bath when we lived here, so I ran a bath for Dad in his gorgeous corner Jacuzzi, but didn't put the plug in.

I switched the television to its highest volume, so it blared out. Dad liked loud noises, they drowned out our screams when he hit us.

The Madam Butterfly record was still on the turntable, he liked this opera a lot, so I left Maria Callas singing on repeat, loud, just as he liked it.

I'd done enough, for now, I didn't want to stay any longer. "Come on Fred, it's time to go."

We left through the front door, slamming it behind us. I heard the family next-door stampede down their stairs as they always did, to peep through their hall window, desperate to know what was happening in our house.

The beat of the music and television pounded so loudly, I thought the walls would shake.

Walking up the path for the last time, holding the front door key in my hand, I headed to the nearby drain covered with a heavy grid and dropped the key between the bars and heard it plop as it sank into the depths of the stinking, germ-laden drain.

My heart pounded as a disturbing flashback raised its ugly head. When I looked into the drain, I could see myself as a three-year-old child, screaming hysterically.

I'd been sitting on the pavement sobbing, next to the grid, wearing my little paisley dress, my hair in bunches.

Minutes before I sat there, I'd gone into the living room, where I stood in shock horror, watching Dad lash out at Mum. Desperately, I positioned myself between them, shoving at Dad's legs, to push him away. "Daddy stop, don't hurt Mummy!" I'd screamed over and over. His muscular legs wouldn't budge, no matter how hard I tried to push him away.

Their hands moved quickly, like in cartoons, which show the blur of speed. Dad lashed out, as Mum tried to defend herself. They moved in rhythm as I got slapped and knocked between them.

Dad noticed me. He pulled me into the air by one arm, then shook me as I screamed for my life and for Mums.

I remembered my cheeks and legs stung because he'd slapped me hard on my bare legs and my apple cheeks, shouting; "shut up, shut up shut up." I was so little and so scared and mummy was sobbing.

Michael was lying in a corner, his head covered by his hands, his body shook. He was five years old.

Overwhelmed, I slipped out of the room, taking my doll Susie with me, away from the chaos, and sat outside on the kerb, not knowing what to do or where to go, all I wanted was for Mummy and Michael to be okay.

The next thing I know is; I'm screaming out for my mummy, but she's running up the path, trying to get away from Dad, as he chased after her, shouting very loudly. He spotted me and immediately turned his attention to me, then yanked me off the pavement, and up under his arm, tightly gripping my small, body, as I fought to make my escape, still clinging on to my baby doll Susie.

Dad yelled; "Helen, get back here," then threw me down next to the dirty drain where I'd just dropped the key.

His nasty face was bright red and twisted, his mouth yelled words I couldn't understand, then he leaped over, and grabbed Susie, out of my little hands, lifted the heavy grid, and dropped her down into the smelly drain where Dad told me big rats and slugs lived, in water, thick with Typhoid. I looked down into the drain for Susie, calling for her but couldn't see her. Dad said the rats had eaten her. I screamed and screamed for my doll. Dad smacked me across my cheeks again, then lifted me and ran back down the road, shouting Mum's name, jostling me painfully. I felt so lost.

Mum reappeared, she went directly to him, pleading with him not to hurt me, but it was too late. At three years of age, I now knew pain and fear, and what it was to be petrified.

Dad dropped me, grabbed Mum, and beat her in the street until she was screaming as hard as I was. She kept trying to get to me, but Dad tugged me away from her, like a starving dog with a bone. Seconds later he shoved me into Mum's open arms and stormed off.

That horrific memory, made me realise Dad hadn't started the abuse when I was seven years old. He'd always done it.

The memories halted as if I had exorcised them. I felt a need to run. so, ran as fast as I could from the bad house, the gossips, the horrible life we'd all endured, and the Dad I didn't want.

We'd wasted too much time here in this miserable house, on this miserable road, this was a dead end. I had to look forward. Dad could rot in his brothel house alone, or with strangers, he was free to choose, but not with us.

Mum, Michael, and I had dreams and aspirations. I was strong, mentally, and physically, as were Mum and Michael. They'd prevented so many terrible things and fought back with a vengeance, they had suffered too much. We had to heal.

I had my life to live, and I knew one day I would find true love. I'd have my own family, whom I would adore. There would be a good man for me. I knew it. People weren't all evil like Dad and his sister. Mr. Evans, Pop, Gran, and Mario had shown Michael, and me there were genuine, good people in this world. But for now, we needed to make up for lost time.

We'd known all along where happiness lived, it was waiting for us on the other side of the door, and we were going to enjoy our lives, on the good side.

"Let's go home Fred, come on," I said, picking up speed, satisfied with my visit.

We ran down the full length of Oak Road for the very last time, laughing and leaping into the air. Fred wagged his tail nonstop, as we headed home.

Mum would be happily gardening now and singing while Gran prepared tea. I expected Michael would be rehearsing on his trumpet, in preparation to take his girlfriend to a concert, one he was playing solo in. I couldn't wait to get home. For now, we had our sunshine back.

END OF BOOK ONE